ALREADY WITHIN

Dedication
I dedicate Already Within *to you,*
the community of souls who have touched my life –
and changed everything.
May you continue to love our damaged hearts and our damaged world
into their true beauty.

Daniel J. O'Leary

Already Within
DIVINING THE HIDDEN SPRING

the columba press
in assocation with
The TABLET

First published in 2007 by
the columba press
55A Spruce Avenue, Stillorgan Industrial Park,
Blackrock, Co Dublin
in association with
THE TABLET PUBLISHING CO
1 King Street Cloisters, Clifton Walk, London W6 0QZ

Cover by Bill Bolger
Origination by The Columba Press
Printed in Ireland by ColourBooks Ltd, Dublin

ISBN 978 1 85607 575 6

Table of Contents

Introduction

There is another way of seeing everything, another way of living our days on this troubled earth. Surprisingly, this vision, this way, is as close to us as our breathing, as intimate as our beating heart. It is like God's secret, unlocked by our surrender to it. It is about trusting in love – and being astonished at what happens. Above all this vision touches us deeply. It is felt in our mind, body, heart and soul.

Our humanity, like that of Jesus, is the womb of the divine. We are all God-carriers, always giving birth to a new vision, forever revealing Infinite Love in the most unlikely places. Already within us, we carry, mostly unknowingly, the fresh wells we thirst for, and the beckoning horizons for which we long. Many people have long been denied that life-changing good news. Yet it is the core of the gospel and is at the heart of our best theology and spirituality. This is a good time to tell the story once again.

The emphasis throughout is on the presence of God in the ordinary moments of people's lives. Each piece in the book begins with a real life-situation and then, at the heart of it, the compassionate presence of an incarnate and unconditionally-loving God is brought to light. This way of seeing things is called the sacramental vision. It is a graced way of parting the veils of the mystery of our complicated lives and of perceiving God at the heart of all creation. It is then we realise that we must love the world more, not less. That is how we save it. And in all our efforts, nothing goes to waste – every effort, every set-back, every daily disappointment and mistake, even temptations and sins – all are transformed. And all are safely harvested.

Blessed are the fearless
You will fear no more once you have faced your own death

Helen knew her weeks were numbered. We had chatted last August about her recurring cancer and about the young family she must soon leave behind. I carefully asked how she coped with her anxiety – and whether I could help in any way. Looking slightly surprised, she said: 'Oh no. I have two lovely children. And a great partner. God has given me time to prepare two little boxes for my sons. One day they will ask their Dad about their mother. In the boxes, I have put a letter for each of them, together with some of myhair, and a small phial of my favourite perfume. I am lucky to have time to do all of this. So why would I be afraid or depressed?'

I often reflect on Helen's words. They have a shocking simplicity about them. They also carry a freedom, a trust and a great courage. For a long time now, the experience of the abundant life, for me, had always to do with freedom from fear. You cannot be truly unafraid until you are unafraid of death. The ultimate courage must lie in the fearless facing of the terrifying unknown. This is why I have been so taken by the amazing words of Helen. As she spoke, the fruits of redemption were already flowering within her.A new level of living had already arrived: a more abundant life. Her essential being was not deserting her; it was being transformed. There was no fear in her face as we talked – only a gentle smile.

Such are the moments of raw courage we remember forever. When Jesus was raised from the dead, all that remained nailed to the Cross was fear. It was fear that crucified Jesus; it is fear that crucifies us. It lies so insidiously deep within us that its compulsive influence is quite unconscious. It presents the negative in the guise of the positive. Fear, not suspicion or hatred, is the opposite to trust and love. To be able to encounter and befriend our fear is to become a new creation, to have our hidden self emerge in delighted living.

Helen left us in November. As we move on into another new year, I tell her story, for January is a month of new beginnings, new risks and resolutions, of what may be called 'courageous conversations' with ourselves and others. It is a time when we are encouraged to bring into focus the latent aspirations of our soul. Whatever relentless urging lies deeply within us, this month is a good time to reflect on what it takes to opt for growth and transformation.

Before embracing new beginnings, we need to be familiar with death. January can be called the month of fear because it is also the month of new possibility. Our inner passion for transcendence and transformation, often felt in January, also brings to the surface the existential fear that we all live with, that dogs every step of our days. Nelson Mandela believes that it is not our inadequacies that make us afraid, but the immeasurable power of our true, graced nature.

How different everything would be if we could speak, act and grow out of passionate conviction rather than stay passive and silent out of a debilitating fear! Those who have met and befriended their fear light up the room and light up the world. They set us all free; they enable us to live our dreams into reality, and, most of all, to tell the truth, though, inevitably, like the Saviour before us, they always pay the price for their courage.

In recent years, I have told the truth more often than I did before. It is a great feeling. It makes you realise how controlled you were, for much of your life, by all and sundry – by memories of your parents' warnings, your neighbours' squinting windows, your priests' sermons of caution, and, if you happen to be a priest like me, by your parishioners, your colleagues and, of course, your poor bishop. It is a pity, I now think, that, especially within our church institution, we are all so fearful of disagreeing with 'authority', of upsetting the status quo, of telling our truth. The layers of control and of internalised fear are tightened around us like an invisible straitjacket. This prison has become so familiar that we do not realise its crippling power, or even its very existence. But, strong as this force is, its opposite is stronger. A heartfelt moment of hope, a whisper of truth, an Easter candle in a window – all are subversive, invincible. Solzhenitsyn said that one courageous word would save the world. So often, however, saying that difficult word is like a mini-death.

Recently, I had the privilege of ministering to another parishioner who died just before Christmas. Edward lingered between life and death for many months. On two occasions I had the opportunity of talking to him about the moment of his imminent death. For some reason or other, I have always thought it to be supremely important for a dying person to be able freely, confidently and consciously to hand over their lives to God. Not everyone has this sacred opportunity, this blessed time, to radically surrender their lives – no matter what the sins, mistakes and failures – into the safe hands of God who cannot wait to embrace and welcome them home.

Like Helen, Edward, too, gave an unforgettable example of the miracles that happen when you face your fear. 'Yes', he whispered, 'yes, I do commit my soul to heaven. I freely trust my life to God. I am ready.' There was, I felt, something eternal, something forever true, something that made death powerless, in those few timeless seconds of no more than a dozen words.

Where does that kind of courage come from? I wondered. Where does it begin? At the hour of our death are we supported and sustained by the hours of our childhood? Do the huge graces of our first years, lost by our compromises, betrayals and original sinfulness, return with faithful destiny to breathe a new dynamic of energy and vitality into us, for another beginning, another journey? A contemporary Greek poet wrote: 'In those fields and streets where you grew up, there you will always live – and die.'

To become the child you were, in the fields and streets you once explored like a young heroine, a daring hero. Is this why Jesus summed up his teaching about eternal life in the symbol of a child? The gifts and graces of our early years are the clearest expression of the nature of God – and of heaven. Maybe, on our deathbeds, they craft the wings of our destiny, to carry us safely home, over the necessary chasms of darkness and light. And maybe, after all, it is not a bed of death, but a bed of life, when immense and unimaginable powers of transcendence are being released.

In a most moving theological poem, Karl Rahner holds that our childhood is not lived through, and cast away, like an outgrown old coat. Rather is it the perennial, eternal heart of our adult lives. We grow into the childhood we once lived through. Even more, this childhood is what we fully recover, possess and celebrate in heaven. And death is the only moment of truth for this transition to take place. 'We do not move away from childhood in any real sense', writes Rahner. 'We move towards the eternity of this childhood, to its definitive and enduring validity in God's sight – a field which bears fair flowers and ripe fruits such as can grow in this field of childhood, and in no other, and which will be carried into the storehouses of eternity.'

Never too late to begin

Every new start is an experience of God in our lives

While the New Year's Janus, the two-faced Roman god of gates and doorways, is always depicted as staring unrelentingly at the past and into the future, our God of Epiphany is embraced as forever creating new possibilities-from within the womb of the present. I like to think of January, my birth month, as the month of courageous beginnings. There is something of the child about January. We sense at this time the stirring of eternal newness. The earth itself seems to be breathing more deeply in anticipation of spring.

Short of nature itself, there is nothing that epitomises the constant condition of readiness for new beginnings more than childhood does. Children's delight in exploring the possible to its limits is the sacrament of God's creative spirit at work in their hearts. In a former parish, St Benedict's, we would remember how, in his famous Rule, the saint spoke to the young hearts of his monks. He began: 'Listen, my child, with the ear of your heart,' and ended, 'With Christ's help, keep this little rule that we have written for beginners.'

In *Crossings*, Mark Barrett OSB quotes Zen Master Suzuki: 'In Japan we have the phrase *shoshin*, which means beginner's mind. In the beginner's mind there are many possibilities; in the expert's mind there are few.'

Beth and Norman are in their eighties. Last January, I visited Norman in hospital after he had damaged his foot while making a frame for one of Beth's paintings. In a matter-of-fact way they asked me to recommend parts of Ireland suitable for their next move. And oh yes, Scotland, Wales or France would be fine too. They wanted to leave Ripon, in North Yorkshire, for somewhere new. I was impressed by their inner freedom. There was something childlike in their plans. And, as I left, Beth called out: 'We could do with a quiet place; I'm learning to play the cello.'

There is something about beginning, or beginning again, that stirs our hearts. The drive towards a new dawn is a pure gift of grace, an experience of God's continuing incarnation in our lives. God makes flesh the divine self every time we die and rise in that tight place between failure and hope. From within his own darkness, the poet Brendan Kennelly wrote:

Though we live in a world that dreams of ending
That always seems about to give in
Something that will not acknowledge conclusion
Insists that we forever begin.

The angels of beginning have no set thresholds through which to enter our lives, but wait at the edge of our experiences, whatever the decade. During any decade it is possible to begin a major voyage to the centre of our identity. Rebecca West reminds us that 'It is the soul's duty to be loyal to its own desires. It must abandon itself to its great passion.' The poet-potter M. C. Richards holds: 'The sin against the Holy Spirit is the sin against new life, against self-emergence, against the holy innerness of each person. It can be committed as easily against oneself as against another.'

Deep down, we are all masters of our own destinies. Whichever way we choose, our decision will have been gradually reached out of a series of small, repeated beginnings along the way of our lives. Even if we have opted too often for the secure, for the burial of that one talent, there is still hope. We are creatures of the light. 'We are God's seed,' preached Meister Eckhart, 'and God's seed must grow into God.' Anais Nin wrote: 'And the day came when the risk it took to remain tight in the bud was more painful than the risk it took to blossom.' But the sad and strange thing is that a point arrives when it is almost beyond us to change and begin again. We have come to believe our interiorised limitations. W. H. Auden observes:

We would rather be ruined than changed
We would rather die in our dread than
Climb the cross of the moment
And see our illusions die.

I remember a story about the pot-bound plant. The roots have nowhere to go but round and round the pot, eventually strangling and choking the plant. They are yearning to find more space and soil, just like our own tired, tangled energies. But no matter how buried our precious lives and dreams, they never die completely. If we don't live life, life will live us. The forces of life and death are so powerful.

There is a quiet desperation in that silent battle when the fingers of first light touch the darkness, when love encounters despair. I once saw a father, with aching despair, look at his wayward son, who had lost out in his battle with drugs. It seemed to me that the father would have given his own life if it stirred that fragile flame to life again within his son's breast. How many mothers must have watched helplessly for the first small blush of health on their desperately ill baby's cheek?

And I remember a student who, unable to face her bulging 'letter-box' of demands, warnings and deadlines, attempted suicide. Standing by her hospital bed, how I longed to infuse her with the spirit and grit I knew she carried somewhere within her. But just then, a new beginning was beyond her. Yet relentlessly, whether faint or fiery, the deeper springs of life will disturb our winter sleep; something greater than our souls will keep attracting their attention. Aquinas defines humans as 'beings that desire' with God's own irrepressible desire within them. In *The Buried Life*, Matthew Arnold wrote:

But often, in the world's most crowded streets,
but often, in the din of strife,
there rises an unspeakable desire
after the knowledge of our buried life;
a longing to enquire
into the mystery of this heart which beats
so wild, so deep in us – to know
whence our lives come and where they go.

January – the month of courageous beginnings. We grow or we die. The poet Goethe urges us: 'Whatever you can do, or dream you can, begin it. Boldness has genius, power and magic in it.'

Beginning requires courage because of the strange forces lined up to prevent it happening. W. H. Murray, the Himalayan hero, wrote: 'Concerning all beginnings there is an elementary truth: that the moment one definitely commits oneself, then providence moves too. A whole stream of events which no man would have dreamt of will happen.' Whenever your heart desires to begin another journey, the whole universe conspires to see you on your way.

Glad New Day

Each morning we can choose the quality of the day ahead

'**D**on't ask her now. She hasn't had her morning coffee yet.' We have all met such people. Maybe we are one of them. Some people are lethal until they get the first 'fix' of the day – a cuppa, a cigarette, the media news. I had a parish priest once, an awkward man – may he rest in peace – who was testy and unapproachable until 10.00 am. He lived by the clock. Each morning, his rising, praying, saying Mass, breakfasting, toileting were invariable. All his movenents were timed by either nature, grace or habit, to the second. You could set your watch by any of them. During those precarious hours we used to circle him carefully, as you would an unpredictable monarch or a wounded lion, until, at the appointed time, he granted his curates a brief window of opportunity for bringing our petitions before him.

Some people are at their best in the moming; others blossom in the late evening; a few give little evidence of any interest at all in the day's proceedings. What we do, think and say, first thing in the morning, the saints tell us, deeply colours the rest of the day. When I was a child we were taught to 'make our Morning Offering'. It was a kind of statement of intent. No matter what, our dawn promise to God would hold true. Once we managed to get it right after we woke up, then everything would be right all day long. In his *Sabbath*, Wayne Muller quotes an old Hasidic poem:

> Take special care to guard your tongue before the morning prayer.
> A person who wakes up in the morning is like a new creation.
> All of your words each day are related to one another.
> All of them are rooted in the first words that you speak.

'We should apprentice ourselves to coming awake,' the poet

David Whyte writes, 'treat it as a form of mastery. The threshold of waking, the entry to the day, is the musician's foot lifted to begin the beat. Miss that beat and you will have to come to a stop, and start again. The dash and flair of the day comes from that foot hitting the floor after the correct restful anticipation. Sometimes a prayerful, painful approach to a difficult day may mean stopping and starting a hundred times, until we learn, like a virtuoso, the thorough, attentive, rhythmic presence of the true musician.'

Fear can ruin our timing – and energy. There are those who dread the arrival of each new day, their stomach already in a knot. The shadows that surface at night continue to haunt us in the light. Too many of us, quietly and hopelessly, wake up to another day of silent despair. Yet every morning provides an opportunity to begin again, to stand on another mountain with a whole new perspective, to refuse to settle for what at first sight seems inevitable. For everyone there is another chance to decide what the day, and the rest of our lives, will be like; a choice about what to set down on the blank page handed to us by each dawn; will it be a sad sequel to yesterday's spent words – or a unique work of art? Every new morning, new week, new year offers us a choice – do we dance it, or do we endure it?

Just as we still struggle with the mystery of how a divine incarnation could happen in an ordinary little baby in a very ordinary place in the course of our ordinary time, so too, even while raising the morning coffee-cup to our lips, we continue to struggle with the shocking belief that the cloud of our fears and despair can be dispersed from our hearts by the healing shaft of light we call God. It is the very ordinariness of the timing of the incarnate God that confounds us.

There is something essentially Paschal about concepts such as newness, beginning, beginning again. Few faiths carry such compassionately repeated opportunities for personal and universal repair, recovery and renewal. And the realisation of this redemption from the night of our fears and losses, can steal into, or slam into, our consciousness while we are busy washing our faces or brushing our teeth. True to the essence of incarnation, the whole economy of our salvation is revealed through the tiny spaces between our fleeting preoccupations. With the precision of a skilled surgeon, God's fingers find the fissures in our attention.

It is difficult to capture in logical prose the divine pleading, the urgent invitation that lies waiting just below the surface of our conscious preoccupations. Like Thomas, we are so slow to believe. Yet this vision, this reality is, no more, no less, what the Christian faith means. Our wildest dreams, which may well be God's dreams too, are within our grasp if, for instance, even between showering and waking the children, we can, with a dogged loyalty, simply utter a heartfelt 'yes'. Another opportunity! 'Life contains a lot of evils,' wrote Atisa in 1007, 'as fragile as a bubble cast up by a wave. How marvellous to wake from sleep still breathing and say "I'm awake! There's still time".' Our souls and bodies will be different then, as we approach the table of our kitchen, the table of our day, the table of our world.

A fierce energy seizes our soul in that innocent moment, the 'Prime' of the monks' Office, when we allow the lover's whisper to vibrate within us: 'With me, this morning, there is nothing you cannot do. I have already examined your day. My love enfolds you; there is no reason to fear.' Is not this what the Christmas we have just celebrated, was about? Is not this inner thrust of personal liberation, and the astonishing conviction that we can transform the world, what our next celebration of Easter and Pentecost will be about as well? 'Why then,' we may ask ourselves as we wait for the windscreen to de-ice, 'do we so limply succumb to the negative charge of our thoughts and feelings?' Capable of achieving all things, every day, in the Saviour who always delivers, we too often settle again for the victim-role, familiar and deadly.

'How we greet the dawn is a measure of the freedom we have made for ourselves,' writes Whyte. 'Freedom in the midst of imprisonment, freedom in the midst of all the catastrophes common to the sins of humankind, the hidden made glorious by sudden vlsibility … One of Blake's most famous engravings is of a young man leaping out of the picture with a great blaze of light behind him, called *The Glad Day*. It carries enormous energy and youthful power, as if the youth is leaping right in our face to ask us what we are up to on this glad day.' I think of the Morning-Christ wrenching us from the tomb of our nights, bringing us to the threshold of a sweet freedom.

Do you ever move into your glad day with the inner authority of that young man? Or feel in your deepest soul the fulfillment of your own promise? Ben Okri writes:

Every day is a new day, a new calendar.
You must begin today to remake
your mental and spiritual world …
Only free people can make a free world.
Infect the world with your light.
Don't be afraid to love or to be loved.
As within, so without.

2/2142730

What is it about Joseph?

There is often one person in our lives who carries the key to salvation

I cannot switch off from Joseph. He has inched his way into my soul. He comes to the presbytery on a Saturday around four. He smells, he shouts, he stares. He is a heavy drinker, a gambler, and has frequent brushes with the law. He barges into every conversation I try to have with parishioners before and after Mass. He mutters obscenities and will not be silenced. He rings me at all hours of the day and night. He wants me to vouch for his purchase somewhere in the city, of a pair of shoes, of a Daniel O'Donnell or Marilla Ness video, of an anorak.

My heart sinks when he presses the doorbell continuously some time before evening Mass. I'm folding the newsletters or snatching a brief nap. He staggers through the door in a storm of blame. 'Celtic should have drawn with Rangers, not beaten them.' (He had bet on a draw.) 'Kieran Fallon should have used the whip in the 2.30.' (His horse came fourth.) 'Fr So and So is turning against me; he told me to get lost last Sunday.' (He had lost a fruitful source of revenue.)

Boundaries have little meaning for Joseph. 'No drinking in the kitchen,' I warn in a hard voice, and Joseph smiles indulgently. 'No shouting during Mass,' and Joseph nods his head understandingly. I have lost my temper with Joseph – often. In my exasperation I have used intemperate language with him that I have deeply regretted. In some kind of extreme frustration I once chased him through the streets around our church to get rid of him – me, desperate; him, stubborn and defiant.

Yet, in spite of all of this, I just cannot understand how Joseph has wrapped himself around my soul. I see him at two levels. On the one hand, I do not judge those who have no time for him. Part of me agrees with those who refuse to have any truck with him. He spends what he gets on drink. His rudeness should not be tolerated in any church. He frightens people and may well dissuade them from coming to Mass. He makes parishioners feel decidedly uncomfortable. Maybe because he reminds them of something in themselves that they find unacceptable.

On the other hand, there is something about Joseph that makes me see him as Jesus Christ. This fact may come across to people as strange or shocking. And it is. But sometimes we misread the raw and uncompromising vision of his mission that Jesus repeated so often. The weekly gathering of the faithful is not meant to be just about a neighbourly, warm meeting of local Catholics. It is more than a parochial, domestic cosiness, worshipping without any sense of sacrifice. It is about a radical turning upside-down of what our respectable society regards as acceptable.

Some months ago, during Mass, I noticed some unusual activity going on down in the body of the church. Joseph had barged through the pews and created quite a racket at the candelabra during the consecration. A few able-bodied worshippers had eased him out into the street. The Mass continued in peace and quiet – with no disturbance, no irritant, nothing but the usual routine.

In one sense, the incident was but a passing moment. And yet I felt it to be a significant one too. I shared my thoughts with the congregation before the last blessing. It comes as a surprise to our parishioners when the counter-cultural nature of the Eucharist is revealed. Its prophetic dimension, almost by definition, has to be rejected. It is too shocking.

Two thousand years on, how can this still be so? After all, we have spent our lives reading and listening to the words of Matthew 25, to the Beatitudes, to the stories about the pharisee and the publican, the cup of cold water. It is one thing to make a fuss over disabled people who are neat and tidy, who call out to our compassion, whose wheelchairs we gladly push while they thank us cheerfully for doing so. Joseph is different. Yet the truly Christian Sunday Eucharist would place him in the front seat. It would honour him as the special guest. It would cherish him as a perfect example of the outsiders in the scriptures – those despised, marginalised and often hated members of a society intent on destroying them. Such are the people that Jesus lived, loved and died for. Such are the people that Jesus placed before everyone else. And such are the people whose feet we, today, are called to wash. Warts and all, Joseph is the litmus test of our faith. He makes me think of this poem by R. A. K. Mason:

His body doubled under the pack
that sprawls untidily on his old back,
the cold, wet deadbeat plods up the track.
The cook peers out: 'O curse that old lag
here again with his clumsy swag
made of a dirty old turnip bag.'
'Hey Cook, bring him in from the gray smelly street;
put silk on his body, slippers on his feet;
give him fire and bread and meat.
Let the fruit be plucked and the cake be iced,
the bed be snug and the wine be spiced
in the old cove's nightcap – for this is Christ.'

Joseph travels a long way to visit us. I often try to fob him off by leaving him in the kitchen with a cup of coffee (three sugars) and a rough sandwich (no cheese). But within minutes he is following me down the corridor, into the sacristy, around the altar. And he is talking, talking, talking – about the price of a pint in The Fox and Hounds, the reduction on chicken curry at Asda, the greyhound, horse or priest who let him down. Joseph is barred from betting-shops, off-licences and video stores all over the city. He spills it all out without embarrassment or guilt.

There is a shocking innocence about Joseph. He may be feckless and reckless but he is not two-faced or devious. I sometimes think he only wants to be listened to, to be respected as a human being, to be understood. Sometimes the veil slips and I have glimpsed this other, tender side of Joseph. Out of the corner of my eye, I have twice noticed Joseph pausing for a moment from his restless ranting and pacing around the church. For some reason his attention was caught by the slanting light on a statue or on the intricate Pugin reredos over the altar. His face changed and he looked as though he was trying to remember something elusive, something from another time, another land – maybe his childhood.

A few weeks ago, after evening Mass, he was once again setting out into the dark to catch his bus 'home'. It was then that Joseph, 'the least of these my people', the butt of the world's jokes and anger, turned to me. 'You know,' he said, a peculiar, impish little smile transforming his ravaged face into its lost youthfulness, 'people miss me when I'm not around. I feel very loved tonight.'

Forging in the Smithy of the Soul
Sometimes we must sweat blood to stay faithful

Lent is here. It stirs something in us – a strange, unsolicited desire. There are intimations of a journey to be made, a river to be crossed, a hill to be climbed. Beyond 'giving something up for Lent' a deeper echo reminds us of a waiting desert. And something tells us that this is a dangerous place to go.

We resist the call into our own mystery, our own depths. We fear further hurting by unknown demons in the barren places. We rightly suspect that our wounds are necessary. There are palaces, we read in the Jewish Zohar, whose gates open only to tears. 'In the desert of the heart let the healing fountain start.'

Some time ago, I arrived in Dublin to do a week's retreat in Lent with a group of priests. A few of them were adamant right from the start that there would be no inner exploring, no revisiting of past hurts; in short, as one put it, 'no digging'. Keep it light please. Talk, yes; feel, no. After the first three days there was still no real breakthrough. I felt a complete failure. It was an experience I will never forget. On Thursday morning the topic was 'The Wounded Healer'. What could I do? I asked two very open and brave members of the group to offer a brief witness to their particular addiction and condition. It was an intensely moving moment. And everything changed. The ice melted. Great work was done during the last few days.

By exposing their own wounds, the speakers enabled the others to open theirs. As Henry Nouwen wrote, we must live them through instead of thinking them through. 'It is better to feel your wounds deeply than to understand them, to let them into your silence. You need to let your wounds go down into your heart. Then you can live them through and discover that they will not destroy you. Your heart is greater than your wounds.'

Instead, we cover the hurts of our hearts with the bandages

of the mind. We bury our painful emotions and think that they are dead. We forget that our presence and personalities are profoundly influenced and shaped by these underground and often violent realities. We live and act out of the invisible shadow-world that turns, silently, within us. Pain needs light. Nothing heals in the dark. Michael Leunig writes,

When the heart is cut or cracked or broken
Do not clutch it, let the wound lie open
Let the wind from the good old sea blow in
To bathe the wound with salt and let it sting.

The scars of Jesus, inside and out, were always there for all to see. He let Mary wash them, Thomas touch them, his mother hold them. He openly wept, openly cursed, openly blessed. He mourned losses with others, he was angry in a crowded temple, he carried his cross in public places. His was a transparent life. And it cost. He was always dying so as to achieve that state. Nothing less will do for us.

Lent perennially pursues the goal of authenticity. The issue is not one of being sinless or perfect - but of being self-aware and integrated. Jesus had no trouble with life's failures, those lost on the margins, or locked in their bad habits. Because for them he came. It was with the hypocrites that he lost his temper. The question that Lent, the season of truth, asks is 'How much reality about yourself can you bear?' Are you aware of your ambiguous motives, your rampant ego, your inner envy, your urge to power? Most of us try to live the Christian life without ever entering those raw and searing cellars of our own unbearable darkness. This avoidance is easy, but costly. Beyond the surface habits of a passionless piety there is a fierce intensity about Lent that relentlessly examines the integrity of our innermost heart.

In *The Divine Milieu* Teilhard de Chardin describes the terror of this surrender to pure, demanding Love: 'At each step of the descent, a new person was disclosed within me of whose name I was no longer sure, and who no longer obeyed me. And when I had to stop my exploration because the path faded from beneath my steps I found a bottomless abyss at my feet and out of it came, arising from I know not where, the current I dare call my life.'

We forever endeavour to short-circuit the relentless call of Christ. We want to equate the increase in our religious behaviour during Lent with growth in holiness. There is, however, no cheap grace. We can weave the notion of Jesus' suffering and death into coats of many colours; we can sing and ritualise 'The Washing of the Feet' and 'The Seven Last Words' – but we are truly lost if we think that these rites alone will ever save our souls. Worship without sacrifice is worthless. So is ritual without painful, personal surrender. We miss the dark truth of Tenebrae.

In our mistaking of the outward ego for the inner essence we are unknowingly denying ourselves the possibility of any radical conversion. We need to face the awful emptiness and nothingness of our lives behind the masks and performances, even the holiest ones. How hard this is to do! 'Forging in the smithy of my soul' is how W. B. Yeats described the hard, inner work of gaining self-knowledge. 'Now that my ladder's gone,' he wrote, 'I must lay down where all the ladders start, in the foul rag-and-bone shop of the heart.'

It is a Lenten grace when we are able to hold within us, as Jesus did, the tension of the paradoxes of our lives. The greater the soul, the greater the shadow. Lent teaches us that we must befriend that shadow, even at great personal cost. Otherwise our soul disintegrates, loses connection. We carry no transforming resonance. We become inauthentic within ourselves, empty before others. Worst of all, we feel false before God.

In Lent we grow by dying. There is no other way. In this dying we recognise the false face we've grown used to, the daily lies we tell, the thoughts of deception that crowd our minds, the infidelities we do not commit only because we might get caught, the lovelessness of our lives parading as shallow compassion, our collusion with conformity, our fear of beauty and big dreams. Nowhere else, but in this awareness of our sins, can we ever be reached and saved. We die to self when we sweat blood to stay faithful, when we sacrifice the ego of our vanity for the essence of our truest being.

This is the dying that daily scrapes the self-renewing fat of pride from the ribs of our soul, bringing a fearless, inner lightness and clarity. When the eye is unblocked, the Buddhists tell us, the vision is sure. This is the liberating dying that puts the truth in our eyes, the resonance in our voice, the power in our presence, the depth in our listening. Since we are now all connected up inside, our heart is no longer divided. Rinsed and cauterised, all that is unauthentic is zapped from our infected being. When the small gods go, God arrives. Heaven, in the end, is where we belong.

With my Body I Thee Worship

Only in the truest emotions of our hearts is God revealed

A few years ago I was called, during the night, to the children's ward at Leeds General Infirmary. A baby had just died. When I walked into the ward the young parents stared at me, and angrily asked, 'Where is this loving God of yours now?' I remember mumbling something about the fact that God was probably crying like they were. But what has stayed with me so clearly is that, ignoring me then, the father took his wife in his arms and said, 'You know I love you.'

I have always felt it such a privilege to be present at that sudden, shy, and emotionally charged moment, when a husband, at the point of tragedy, tenderly whispered those words of life. It is unforgettable because it is so real, so true and therefore so sacred. My understanding of Incarnation now is that such moments are the only ones in which God can touch and hold us, redeem and save us, console and empower us. The way the Word-become-Flesh heals and restores happens in no other situation than in the human interplay of senses, emotions and physical relationships.

In a deadly dualism, we find it so difficult to accept the revelation that it is God's delight to be worshipped in the way we touch and look at each other, in the way we listen and talk to each other, in the way we forgive and promise to start all over again. Instead we seem to have erected a separate holy edifice, an institutional locus, for God's encounter with us to happen, for the divine intimacy to take place.

Where else is there to experience the abundant life promised by Jesus if not in the trust and encouragement of those who love us, in the almost impossible words of forgiveness from those we have hurt, in the sacrifices we make to stay faithful to our partners? Our senses and emotions, our most intimate feelings, our wildest aspirations and our deepest despair, our sins and our failures – such are the only moments in which our incarnate God can be intimate with us. Is this not the reason behind Karl Rahner's famous definition of sacraments as 'celebrations of what is already there in human experience'?

The senses have rightly been called the thresholds of the soul. They are the only means we will ever have for feeling the embrace of God's joy and relentless trust in us. In the sacrament of marriage, where human love is revealed to be divine love in disguise, we have such a shining example of the sacredness of our humanity. It is where people set each other free, release the creativity and beauty in each other's hearts, give permission to each other to be truly themselves. 'With my body I thee worship' (from the Ritual) is, at the same time, a human promise, a divine prayer and a potentially graced experience of God's essential delight.

But if you dare to love be prepared to grieve. The mystery of pain and death that we tend to apply only to the Christ of Good Friday is daily played out in every marriage across the world. Only in the cauldron of our emotions, when we are over-whelmed by the forces within us, have our doctrines, liturgies and scriptures any real meaning.

For many Christians, this understanding of our church is too beautiful to be easily believed. Most people do not understand the fleshing of the Word to mean that now the experience of God has to do with the body as well as the soul, with the kitchen as well as the cathedral, with physical pleasure as well as spiritual pain, with human passion as well as contemplative prayer.

Instead of relentlessly trying to drag the 'secular' experiences of marriage into the territory of the church, the church's role, in truth, is to rejoice and embrace the divine love and meaning already within the magic and mystery of the way human beings love, create new life and say 'sorry' to each other. The daily 'ordinariness' of married life is the human presence of God in every home. We must strive to become more, not less, human. The eucharistic challenge is to keep reminding us of this mystery – to keep redeeming and naming each passing moment as a place of grace, a little epiphany, in a place that is already the body of God.

In his book, *Living Love*, Jack Dominian writes: 'We live in an age where relationships are considered the supreme expression of being human. Christianity has to recognise this reality by acknowledging that sanctification is to be found in the love present between people ... the world lives this truth in a shadowy,

unclear way. But it knows that there is something sacred about relationships ... the world may not trust the churches, but everyone trusts genuine love because, however wounded we are in
our personalities, we all have a sense of what it means, and we
hunger for it.'

He is right. There is a persistent suspicion of 'mere' humanity
that has poisoned all our recent efforts at promoting the dream
and revelation of Jesus Christ. True evangelisation will only
ever really happen right where people and passions storm and
whisper, love and fear, hurt and heal. God's love is not lessened
when human love is raised. Nor is the church diminished when
the table and bed of the marital home are regarded as altars to
God's glory, too. In fact the Eucharist serves only to sift and
save, to reap the harvest of all that happens in the life of a family.

And then the definition of the home as the 'domestic church'
takes on a whole new depth and vibrancy. It is in the agony and
ecstasy of marriage, in the infinite heights and depths of human
minds, bodies and souls that the mysterious potential of human
love is played out. And there, and there only, is played out too
the tenderness, compassion and continual fleshing of our lovely
God.

There is a most beautiful theology of marriage waiting to be
explored. Karl Rahner emphasises that without the previous celebration of the raw reality of life and marriage, the subsequent
celebration of the sacraments in church will be devoid of meaning. Without the lived life of love, first, our liturgies are empty.
The thresholds to heaven are opened only from our earth. And
every single moment of our ordinary and extraordinary lives are
the first rungs of this Jacob's ladder. There is no other place to
encounter God; no other place for God to encounter us. It is all of
a piece. Everything belongs. Ordinary miracles can be daily encountered. Sacred liturgy reveals, purifies and celebrates the
divinity of every act of love.

We have forgotten that God can only love us through the
human heart. When the young father clasped his dead baby in
one hand, and held his weeping wife with the other, what a
supreme struggle between love and death went on inside him.
Accepting the overwhelming tragedy of the death of his dreams,
he could still tenderly whisper tremulous words of life into his

distraught wife's heart. In a hundred lifetimes could there ever
be a more searing, intimate glimpse of the human power of God
made flesh?

Wisdom in a Kiss

How a tiny baby's embrace makes sense of the cross

There is something about Good Friday that I cannot get used to. It always comes into our lives so strangely new. It is more than the quietness of our small city of Ripon or of the stillness of the fields that stretch out towards the Yorkshire Dales. It is as if creation itself participates in some kind of turning of the light – a light that touches the heart of each person, and even of the cosmos itself. There was a brooding presence about the tradition of *Tenebrae* which many of you will remember. To be a part of that ominous moment, to capture some of that universal mystery requires our stillness, our openness and a surrender that is rare enough.

I remember a Good Friday afternoon watching our parishioners remove their shoes and file slowly towards our hand-held cross at the altar. One by one, young and old, they reverently pressed their lips, in a gesture of intimacy, against the cold comfort of this bronze symbol of pain. I was moved anew at the mystery happening before me, at the depth of a faith that could perennially draw people into such a rich and profound ritual. How could they embrace this symbol of death? How could they kiss the very source of the destruction of a God made human? And in doing so, how could they meet, greet and welcome all the destructive elements in their own lives?

On this dark day, how amazing it was, how full of terror and beauty, of graced insight, that we publicly and deliberately, mostly blindly but yet hopefully, knelt down in adoration before the gaping wounds of love that destroyed the One who saved us, and that are still kept open and bleeding by our infidelity and our sins?

As I watched the shuffling queue, something inside me lurched. For one reason or another, in my heightened state of awareness, I could identify the trials and traumas of so many of our community, as they humbly waited their turn to kiss the cross. I noticed a man who had told me he had lost his faith. (And then I remembered a bishop I met in the United States in 1999. He told me about the daily agonies he endured while going through the motions of ministering to his flock, knowing that, in his heart, he believed in nothing any more.) I prayed for them both.

The queue continued. A man in a wheelchair; a woman with crutches. I partly envied them. Their crosses were visible; mine were invisible. The source of their pain was, in a sense, outside them; mine was within. So I prayed for all those disabled inside, like me.

There the parishioners were, shuffling along in silent sorrow. I knew so many of their stories: a couple whose children had gone astray and the self-blame they heaped upon themselves; a husband who could not forgive his wife's infidelity, neither could they regain any harmony together, and so, for them, the days and nights of living hell burned in an ordinary house in an ordinary street.

Perhaps it was inappropriate, but I continued to drift from my presider's role into my own inner world. I realised, a little deeper than I already had, that, one way or another, we are all spiritually and emotionally crippled. At some level and at certain times we are all, as Henry Thoreau said, leading lives of quiet desperation. I wept inwardly for the world of pain, but I wept, too, for myself. Is it possible, I wondered, as a priest, to be the most religious person in the parish and yet to be the least spiritual? Nobody is more susceptible to being trapped by the trappings of religion than the priest himself.

It was at this point that I wanted to throw off the weight of the vestments I was wearing and reveal my raw, trembling spirit. What else, I wondered, is today's ritual of shadow and death about, if it does not touch the deepest part of my own sinful, fragile soul?

These days, most priests will confess to feeling the icy grip of fear around their hearts. Many of us inwardly rage against the way we are currently perceived and treated by those we serve. 'Ecce homo,' I wanted to shout, 'I'm not a clerical machine, a clone of the institution; I am, like Jesus, a man, a human being, with needs and cravings and desires to express myself and to be free.'

It was then that I noticed a young mother with her small child waiting in the queue. She knelt down and kissed the cross. She then lifted her baby so that her tiny mouth would meet the hard nail sticking out from the feet of the cold, dead Jesus. My heart contracted. Why? I'm not sure. I think I saw, in an instant, the future life of this small baby. In some unusual way I felt the inevitable pain that lay ahead in the destiny of this child. And then the pathos, the heart-wrenching pathos of that tiny kiss, when, all unknowing (or maybe not!), with a fierce wisdom that defies the sophisticated doctrines of a thousand religions, this little creature instinctively embraced the dark shadows that would, somehow, one day, break her and make her, hurt her and heal her, and then, as Jesus promised, guide her way to heaven.

Was this her first 'yes', I wondered, to the inevitable paradox of being in love with God, to the necessity of pain for new life to happen, to the mystery of the womb and the tomb that she had participated in, a year or two earlier, at the moment of her birth and baptism? In some mysterious way that we will never understand, maybe some instinct in her wise wee heart already knew that 'if you dare to love, you must be prepared to grieve'.

It was now time to prepare the altar for Holy Communion. Many thoughts around this afternoon's ritual came into my head as we processed to the sacristy for the ciborium. Teilhard de Chardin said that if we could but gather together, in one instant, all the suffering of our lives, the explosion of love would transform the whole world. The mystics hold that our love-filled pain is the fuel for the journey towards enlightenment. The Buddhists advise us to use suffering to end suffering. The Jewish Zohar tells us that the gates of the Holy Palace open only to human tears.

As I climb the altar steps it occurs to me that it isn't really the cross that we kiss; it is the love that shaped it. It is not by the suffering of Jesus that we are redeemed. We are saved by his love, not his cross. What we are really kissing is the living, loving flesh of a passionate and beautiful man, not the bleeding wounds so callously inflicted on him by his thoughtless persecutors.

That, incidentally, is the precious revelation which Mel Gibson has missed in his *The Passion of the Christ*. The film is about the happenings of the first Good Friday, and is already having a huge influence around the world. The production is theologically flawed. The emphasis is in the wrong place. Shocking brutality can never save us. Only love redeems. And the focus of redemption today is the bloody body of Christ that we call our beautiful, broken world. Why do I suspect that in some mysterious way, the little child I noticed last Good Friday carried the whole truth of Christ's passion in her brief and fragile life. So great a wisdom in so small a kiss!

On the Pulse of our Wounds
'In the middle of my winter I discovered an invincible summer'

It was when the evenings were lengthening in the first week of the new millennium that Laura's long lashes began to move again. During those months of waiting, there had been a paleness about her, like a sick baby, and her parents' faces had become etched for ever with pain and fear. It had been a long Good Friday for the Connolly family.

One day, Bruce's artistic passion was no longer there. The urge to paint had left him. He looked helpless, without light in his eyes, without fire in his belly. It was a great loss, a deadly emptiness, 'like something torn out of me', he said. For most of a year we waited. The autumn turned to winter. Then, around this time last year, at a Vigil Mass, I noticed, when he came to receive Holy Communion, a small, shy smile on his face. It was all we needed to know. For Bruce, spring had come.

It was to reveal the grace in moments such as this that Jesus died. It was to identify the hands of a healing God in those small resurrections that Jesus was raised from the tomb. Whenever we weep tears of relief, gasp at the endurance of someone's commitment to duty, wonder at the power in one word or look of love, then we are coming down from the cross of defeat. Whenever we keep going in spite of the deadly, daily routine of trivial chores, fight the despair that lurks in our breasts, refuse to become embittered when betrayed, then we are living out, in space and time, the hard-won fruits of our Saviour's passion.

If resurrection does not impinge and impact on the nitty-gritty moments of our days and nights then, whatever else it may be, it is not real for us. It does not, to be sure, deliver us from the brokenness of being human, but it does put us back together again. The continual miracle is to be discovered precisely within the ordinary, relentless repetitions of each week, sometimes unobtrusively, sometimes with a shock. A father holds his fearful son as he momentarily turns back, in panic, just before stepping on to the rugby pitch for his first match, against lads twice his size. 'Don't be afraid,' the father says. 'We know you can do it.' A woman holds her trembling man in the middle of the night and whispers: 'Shh, love; it will soon be light.'

If these words are not God's words, twice divine by virtue of nature and grace, of birth and baptism, then where do we look for the meaning of being saved and redeemed? Or is there another world somewhere, where Easter happens, but not in a way that can be 'proved upon the pulses', as the young poet Keats asked before he died at twenty-five? When that father, and that lover, spoke their words of hope to the beloved of their hearts, they were doing exactly what Jesus did: no more, no less, whenever he uttered those self-same words of ultimate salvation before and after his final, Paschal breakthrough. What was revealed at Easter is that every human act of love is a divine act of love: that God, too, looks excitedly through our eyes, whenever we look at anybody or anything with wonder and delight.

The essence of Easter is that it changes everything. A new reality has entered into our consciousness. Nothing, any more, is irrevocable. The impossible has become possible. Betrayal, loss of innocence and despair do not have the last word. Because now, the many graves and prisons we live in can be regarded as the very source of an amazing freedom – transforming our lives into new levels of light and being. There is a breath-taking moment when we begin to realise that the past does not matter any more, that a totally new page can be turned over every morning for us to write on. But to turn that new page we must often reach beyond the limits of possibility, into the depths of our soul.

In fairly recent Western art, the Easter mystery is often depicted in pictures of the rising Christ carefully and confidently stepping out of some kind of coffin or tomb. It is all very deliberate and controlled. The Eastern Orthodox traditions reveal another story. The 'harrowing of hell' is a theme in their mosaics and frescoes. In them our Saviour is portrayed as bursting out of the fires of damnation in the most dramatic and amazing way. Clutching Adam and Eve (the human race) under each arm, he thunders through the gates of Hades, from the inside out.

He is not painted as stretching to reach them, or drawing them up, or sending down a ladder. No, he vanished into the red-hot heart of hell, the place where the burning is most intense, those aching places in all our lives where pain runs rampant. With a fierce look in his eyes, his face blazing with intense desperation, he bursts out of the jaws of death, grasping close his precious bundles, with chains and locks and prison bars flying off in all directions. That's the total intensity we're in danger of losing. That's the cost of discipleship. Easter is not for the faint-hearted.

What's important to remember is that such effort, such total commitment, is continued in the unpredictable hours of our own days, in the violence of our passions, in the power of our compulsions, in the relentless urges of the mystery of our being. Wild and wayward emotions suddenly rise from deep within us. They strike us, without warning, in the stirrings and yearnings that come to us, with a devastating clarity, during the course of a normal day. They steal upon us at night when we dream, for no apparent reason, about people we have loved, feared, longed for, neglected or hated, bringing aching realities back to life, leaving us very unready for the coming day.

The intense Good Friday of love and fear, of hope and despair, is again lived through, whenever we try to hold the space between faithfulness and betrayal, telling the truth and telling lies. Holding that ambiguous space is a holy art. On the cross, with outstretched arms, Jesus did it. On the one hand, his doubt, despair, a cursing thief and the absence of his father. On the other hand, his faith, his hope, a blessing thief and the presence of his mother. And already, within this night of contradiction, within this threshold of anguished waiting, the light was gathering itself to dance, in the morning, on the mountains. The seeds of the one were already taking root in the soil of the other. As we can gather from John's gospel, the whole three traumatic days of Holy Week were, for Jesus, experienced in one timeless moment.

It is the same with us. For God is always true to the essence of incarnation. Whether gently or dramatically, it is only to the extent that we have sensed the presence of a redeeming Easter 'on the pulse' of the wounds of our mortality, that we can ever claim heaven.

Maybe resurrection, as our ultimate future, will be the surprised realisation that we have been experiencing it, at least in part, all our lives. We will know well when we're home.

'Heaven', wrote Harry Williams in *True Resurrection*, 'will be recognised as a country we have already entered, and in whose light and warmth we have already lived.'

The Mothering Landscape
The sacramental view from a Mass on a mountain

This is the time of year when nature beckons to us, the high roads call to us, something stirs in our soul. Shades of Druidic customs awaken within Celtic hearts. On St Patrick's Day a few years ago, I said Mass on top of the Paps. I was born and grew up in their shadow in the south-west of Ireland. The Paps are two breastshaped mountains that dominate the skyline along the road that runs from Cork to Killarney. They are named in honour of the goddess Danu (*Dhá Chíoch Danann*) who reigned supreme across Europe in more peaceful times.

It was at the request of the local people that I celebrated the Eucharist on the Paps that spring morning, remembering how the light of Christianity and the shadow of paganism have chased each other delightedly down the centuries of worship. They still do. As we hit the summit of the Western Pap, the *ceo draíochta*, the magic mist of folklore parted, and we caught a glimpse, with the inner eye, of what Kathleen Raine calls 'the bright mountain behind the mountain'.

But just behind, and through the thinnest surface,
Not uncreated light or deepest darkness,
But those abiding essences the rocks and hills and mountains,
Are to themselves, and not to human sense.

Reared within a few miles of the Paps, our finest scholar of things Celtic, Dr Noel O'Donoghue, writes of an imagination in touch with transcendent truth and beauty, with the world of the senses and the light of memory:

Those who see the mountain spiritually are constantly conscious of presences behind what they see and hear and touch, somehow interfused with the colours of dawn and sunset, somehow seeking communication through the voices of the winds and the voices of the many waters, through the touch of the air and the mosses and the peat fields underfoot, through the scent of broom and bog-myrtle, the taste of clear bright water and wild strawberries.

I have little doubt that a profound transcendence was happening in the silent hearts of that faithful gathering. Here, I felt sure, was a breathtaking moment of sacramental imagination. As we recalled the sacred mystery of life and death on those timeless rocks, and lifted high the bread and wine of our history and destiny, something in us knew that we were completing a love-song that had started here 4,000 years before. It had always been a holy mountain. But now we were eating and drinking another kind of salvation, not on the pagan breasts of a divine goddess but on the broken body of a Servant-King.

Our Mass on the Paps stirred the unconscious memory of those who climbed the mountains that day. The pagan and Christian within all of us embraced again. Maybe our simple celebration that morning did something to heal and complete everything within us and around us that was broken and unfinished.

Away to the west of us the Atlantic Ocean sang of God's vastness; to the east, the Golden Vale of Munster reflected God's bounty. High overhead, wandering across the perfect sky, a little family of stray clouds was a sacrament of humanity's lonely pilgrimage in search of home. All of us, I'm sure, in that sacred space, were connecting with unspoken, unspeakable dimensions of our being.

And then I spoke the words of divine disclosure and universal revelation: 'This is my Body.' Those words seemed to reverberate around the earth like the angels' Christmas song and to echo off the rim of the sun with transforming power. They were first whispered by our Creator when the world was brought to birth; again, when the Word became human, and now, a thousand times a day, when people around tables receive the sacrament of 'who they already are'. 'This is my Body.' It is God become atom, become galaxies, become universes, become earth, become flesh, become everything. It is too much for us to understand, too much to hold: how in wine and wafer, in imagination and faith, we could touch, for a fleeting but timeless moment, something of the mystery of death and life!

It was this, we said, that moved us most. It seemed to us that the play and struggle between the dying and rising, the hope and despair, in the loving heart of all God's people, and in the living cosmos itself, were purified and celebrated with, as Dr

John Macquarrie puts it, 'a directness and an intensity like that of the Incarnation itself '.

John Moriarty, a philosopher and mystic who was also reared in the shadow of the Paps, refers to the deceptive sensuality of the *Dhá Chíoch Danann*. 'Not that their sumptuousness is the whole story,' he writes, 'For one thing, the nipples of these divine breasts are cairns; they are tombs suggesting that even while we are undergoing the disintegrations of death we are, for all that, being divinely nurtured.'

And there they were, standing or kneeling around me, men and women of the mountains, heads bowed and backs erect, farmers' families from the fragile fields of their livelihood, their weather-wise hearts so well acquainted with the harsh and healing seasons of their lives, living sacraments of the human need to survive, to give thanks and to adore. A new understanding blessed us that morning as I read out Teilhard de Chardin's dynamic reflections in his 'Mass on the World':

> I will place on my paten, O God, the harvest to be won, this morning, by the renewal of daily labour. Into my chalice I shall pour all the sap that is pressed this day from the fruits of the earth ... All the things of the world to which this day will bring increase; all those that will diminish; all those that will die. This is the material of my sacrifice.

John Paul II adds significantly to these soul-stirring insights: 'The incarnation of God the Son signifies the taking up into unity with God not only human nature, but in this human nature, in a sense, everything that is flesh ... the incarnation then, also has a cosmic significance, a cosmic dimension; the first-born of creation unites himself with the entire reality of man, within the whole of creation.'

Later, in *Ecclesia de Eucharistia*, in a supreme moment of pure sacramental imagination, the Pope continued: 'Yes, cosmic!' he wrote, 'Because even when the Eucharist is celebrated on the humble altar of a country church, it is always, in some way, celebrated on the altar of the world. It unites heaven and earth. It embraces and permeates all creation.'

Wondering about these things is another way to celebrate St Patrick's Day.

And a Celtic reflection for Mothers' Day: My wish for you, our mother readers, is that your children may one day bless and honour you for the fire of inner conviction that you light in their hearts. One Mothers' Day evening, not long before she died, using my Irish name, my own mother placed this Scottish Celtic blessing on my pillow:

Be thine the encompassing of the God of life;
Be thine the encompassing of the Christ of love;
Be thine the encompassing of the Spirit of grace,
To befriend thee and to aid thee,
O Donal of my breast;
To befriend thee and to aid thee,
Thou beloved of my heart.

Easter at the Forge Cross

Resurrection is about the passion for the possible in our everyday lives

L ike a recurring dream, it comes back to me every Easter
week – a vivid memory that seems to have lodged deep
within me, and only emerges on a sunny afternoon in
April. I'm about fourteen years old and just up after a teenage
type of flu. I'm walking along the Forge Cross road near my
home in Ireland. A spring sun is shining. I'm wearing a new
brown suit and new brown leather shoes. To my right is John
Sullivan's sloping field. To my left, the railway line that runs by
the banks of the Collabha. And throughout all the decades of my
life, I still feel in my body that strange and lasting delight in
being so vibrantly alive.

Now why should that moment have stayed with me so vividly?
What timeless thing was happening that afternoon, half a century
ago, that buried itself in my loins and soul, to be awakened by
the sun at the same time every year? Whatever it was – this inde-
scribable and transforming emotion – I see it now as some kind
of experience of Easter, of the abundant life. It was an Emmaus
moment, of a burning heart in an awakening human being.

From an early age, I have always wondered about how physical is the presence of God, how real is the actual effect of salvation on my life. What is the tangible impact of the Incarnation,
of being redeemed, of being a new creation? How does it affect
the way I walk and talk and listen, the way I live and move and
have my being? How does it transform the way I am present to
everything, to my gifts and shadows, to those I fear and admire,
to the terrible sounds and sights of human destruction in a
weeping world?

During the second half of my life, these questions have never
left me. As I participate in the lives of our parishioners here at St
Wilfrid's, there are endless witnesses to the transforming power,
in the here and now, of the Paschal Mystery. And at Mass every
Sunday, wherever appropriate, I draw attention to these experiences of Resurrection, to the places of grace. The overcoming of
a fear or an addiction is surely the felt presence of the Risen

Christ. So, too, is every truly new beginning after the healing of the hurt of a divorce, of a betrayal or deception. Such amazing breakthroughs, I point out, are stunning miracles of grace.

Resurrection is as earthy, local and intimate as our sweat and blood, our dreams and nightmares, our drives and passions. It is as real as whatever or whoever drives and drains us, draws and drags us. Resurrection, in fact, is the deepest meaning of everything that brings a smile to our faces, a tear to our eyes, a vitality to our bodies, a softness to our voices and a tenderness to our touch. Resurrection is as real as that.

Last Sunday, after Luke's Easter gospel, I waited on the lectern and looked at the people. At such timeless moments I can sometimes feel the relentless rhythms of their hearts – the murmur of harmony or the turbulence of conflict. This awareness fills me with wonder. These are the times that I see, with a painful clarity, the utter fallacy of the dualism that underpins so much of our teaching, preaching and evangelising. There are no longer two realities, the mystery of Easter convinces us – one 'merely human', the other holy; one the church, the other the world, one human, the other divine. In the baby-body of the Incarnation, in the destroyed body of the Crucifixion, in the shining, human body of the Resurrection – that is the same body in which all dualism has been transcended. To be truly human, it is now established, is to be divine. To be is to be blessed. To live is to be holy. Everything is grace.

To believe this is to be transformed into another way of perceiving our identity and our humanity. To believe this is to be subjected to a paradigm shift where we are present to ourselves and to others in an irrevocably transformed way. A veil parts. The stone is moved. The focus changes. In light of this disclosure moment, I found it so moving to believe that the lifeless and vibrant, the full and empty, the struggling and hoping people before me last Sunday, were, without doubt, the very heart of the church, the blessed sacrament of the divine presence, the only true and real presence of the living Christ of the Resurrection. God comes to us disguised as our lives. Nothing is just ordinary any more. Every bush is a burning bush. This incredible revelation is, in fact, the very mystery we celebrate at every Eucharist.

At the end of Lent we read, 'See, I am doing a new thing. I am sending a fresh stream through the desert.' The Resurrection promises that the dry places will always burst into vibrant life, that the stone will always be rolled away, that nothing good stays dead for long. Every dream can be stirred into life, every fire re-kindled. To be sure, we all carry small graves of cynicism and despair within us. Most of us are acquainted with demons of guilt, shame and sadness. The stunning revelation of Easter is that this winter is all over.Without exception and for ever. There is no sin, loss, betrayal or despair that is final. All we have to do is to choose life, forgiveness and compassion. Small wonder that the Celts of old saw the sun dancing over the mountains on Easter morning.

The sun should dance for us, too. Everything is now new and fresh. Our lives are transformed.We have just come through the amazing ceremonies of Holy Week. At the Vigil, there is a deliberate assault on the senses, those senses that we call the thresholds of the soul. It is all intensely physical, emotional and spiritual. Every liturgical stop is pulled out to ensure that we do not forget the glimpse we have been given of the meaning of the mystery. Easter then, like Christmas, like Baptism, like Eucharist, is the celebration of the body in its wholeness set free – that human, sacred body of ours which is the temple of the Holy Spirit, and which will live, in its entirety, with the still-shining, wounded body of Jesus in heaven, for ever.

During this Easter week, we are called again to those threshold-senses of ours by the church in a most extraordinary way, when the story of the strong physical presence of Jesus, holding the bread and wine over the table in the tavern, explodes the Emmaus-bound disciples from their doubt, and, before that, provides the same release, when the probing finger of the doubting Thomas explores the broken skin of the still-human Christ. Like him, we must dare to believe. In last week's newsletter I asked any struggling parishioners, as they drifted towards the distractions of Emmaus, to imagine the following life-giving whisper coming from the living gospel within their hurting hearts:

I am the Spirit of the Risen Christ. If you dare to believe it, I can set free the dance in your body, the music in your soul, the dream in your heart. You can overcome every fear – with me: you can forgive every hurt – with me: you can make your life a journey of wonder – with me. With your bodies you can worship each other – with me. Every hope you carry inside you can come true – because with me you can do all things. You can mend a broken world because now, everything is possible. Heaven on earth lies open before you today for the taking. But there is one condition to this glorious transformation – of you, of humanity and of all creation – you must dare to believe it.

A Hard Line won't Do

'Tenderness comes from long looking'

A few years ago a shy young couple from a 'good Catholic family' in the parish asked to get married in church. I had never seen them at Mass and so I did not immediately agree to their request, and suggested further meetings. Maybe it was the tone of my voice, or maybe they were not very keen in the first place, but the outcome was that I never saw them again. I did hear some subsequent comments about the parish priest being 'a hard man'. That still hurts. I regret taking the stance I did. Even though the vast majority of the priests with whom I shared this moment have wholeheartedly agreed with me, I now know, in my heart, that I was wrong.

In my travels since then, I have listened to a great number of bruised Catholics who find it difficult to understand the 'hard line' that so many of us priests take, especially with regard to the reception of the sacraments. I remember attending a meeting for episcopal vicars in the nineties in London. Someone suggested a wider use of general absolution and a more generous attitude towards many of those no longer allowed to receive Holy Communion. 'Good God!' one of those present exclaimed, 'If we go down that road our churches will be crammed with sinners every Sunday morning!'

Many older priests regret, like I do, the times that we have taken the tough option with fragile parishioners. To be sure, we do need some kind of guidelines so that our communities can stay in line with the vision of Jesus. And we do look for agreed diocesan policies and procedures about pastoral practice from time to time. But what the more experienced pastors will now freely admit – especially those who are in their later decades and who are risking the inner, spiritual journey into their own soul – is that they have stopped sticking to the party line when that line is less than compassionate. They regret the times they have placed restrictions on the unconditional love of God. They no longer shrink divine mercy to the size of their own timidity and fear. God's extravagant compassion reaches well beyond the boundaries and categories of prescribed behaviour, of our knowledge and certainties.

The bishops of England and Wales, at one of their meetings a few years ago in the north of England, admitted in their 'Lakes Meditation' that they were probably excluding from the Eucharist the very sinners to whom Jesus would have given pride of place. Am I right in thinking that much of the present-ation of our faith in recent decades, the general tone of many Vatican curial documents, even the weekly thrust of many of our homilies and catechetical content, are still tinged, if not deeply coloured, by an attitude of admonition and caution? 'The dan-gers of life are many, and safety is one of them,' wrote Goethe.

My abiding concern is about the loss of the reassuring invit-ation of a beckoning God, as revealed so unambiguously in the life of Jesus. Jesus was so good at simply walking with people without judging them, liberating people without making them dependent, forgiving people unconditionally while saving their embarrassment. He set out only to bless people with their own divine power.

Above all, the delight of Our Saviour was, as Emily Dickinson put it, 'to dwell in the potential of human beings'. This is what he was doing on the road to Emmaus. He was clari-fying for his faithful friends what they already half knew. He didn't berate them for their slowness, but because he loved them he was prepared to wait for their hearts to understand. Like all true teachers, he could recognise the butterfly in a caterpillar, the eagle in an egg and the saint in a sinful human being. And, as the sun coaxes open the petals of the daisy on a spring morning, so too the love of Jesus reached into the uncertain hearts of those who found themselves drawn to him.

There is a story about a flower that blooms only in the dark. Not only is this unexpected moment unseen; the aroma, too, is seemingly wasted in the night air. The light of God in our hearts is something similar – shining within our darkest night and our besetting sins. Not many are aware of this extraordinary, para-doxical epiphany. It was the way of Jesus to remember this divine truth and instead of condemning, blaming and judging, his gen-tleness touched every heart that lay open to him.

Knowing his own temptations and emotions, he understood those of others. Familiar, through contemplation, with the labyrinth of contradictions in his own soul, he saw accurately into the mysteries of the human heart. And, in the same manner, without enough silence in our own deepest selves, we ministers of the church will continue to alienate people by too much projected control and too little graced trust.

What the churches need to recover is the tenderness of Jesus. This only comes, as the poet Roethke said, 'from long looking'. We would do well to reflect on how patiently a mother entices out the humanity and the personality of her baby. Hans Urs von Balthasar, theologian of beauty, wrote: 'After a mother has smiled for a long time at her child, the child will begin to smile back. She has awakened love in its heart, and in this awakening love, she awakens also recognition.' And Rilke said that an infant's journey into human awareness depended on the beckoning, beguiling voice of the mother, easing the child into selfhood, lessening the shadows of the abyss that trap us in inarticulate darkness. You could hardly say, in light of this reality, that the mother takes 'the hard line' with her baby. Yet Mother Church, with her children, too often does.

To return to my opening confession of tough pastoral practice, I hardly encountered that young and loving couple as a mother would her baby. I do not think it makes me soft or sentimental to hold that, as heralds of the gospel, lay and clerical, we now need to recover that mother tongue, that coaxing, patient and captivating presence with which our own mothers, and before that Jesus, made us aware of our own amazing mystery.

We live in a terrifying world. There is so much fear and darkness all around us. Too often we feel small and powerless. In our heart of hearts, when we are alone at night, when we let down the masks, the front, the brave smile, what we long for is not the precise language of official church-speak; we yearn for the warmth, the loving eyes and the open arms of our mother. As anyone who is familiar with the emotions of those who feel alienated in hospices, neglected in residential homes and frightened in our hospitals knows, what we all want, at the end of the day, is to be welcomed home.

Caught between earth and heaven
The astonishing story hidden in the Silent Saturday

I have always felt a strange emptiness around the church, and an ache within me, each Holy Saturday morning. It is like a suspension of time after our intense experience of Good Friday's trauma. It is as though everything is put on hold in that still, slow moment between two powerful liturgies with their soul-sized re-membering. Small wonder I have felt uneasy. The quiet non-time of these first hours after his death concealed perhaps the most intense of all Jesus' conflicts – his naked encounter with the raw powers of hell, so that his father's beloved creation would soon be liberated.

Holy Saturday – the forgotten day, yet the most amazing day of destiny. On Holy Saturday last year I felt the need to be alone. As huge, late petals of snow gathered on the just-opened cherry blossoms throughout Yorkshire, I headed for Scarborough. I wanted to be near something vast; something that hinted at mystery. As I watched the long, rolling waves that stretched from the old Roman Signal Station in the north to the South Bay, I reflected on the meaning of this 'longest day', that dark space where the tomb becomes the womb, that uncertain time when the light creeps in.

Could it be, I wondered, that instead of preparing to leave the tomb and the earth behind him, and returning to heaven, his work completed, Jesus was still accomplishing his most precarious mission? We are free to speculate on the prediction of Jesus in Matthew's gospel about spending three days in the heart of the world so as to inhabit it intensely, and drive it forward from within. Maybe Jesus did not step out of the tomb and head for heaven. Maybe he went deeper into the broken reality of life, where death itself is so powerful, so as to redeem it from within. Having once become human in the body of his mother Mary, he now actually becomes the whole world in a more comprehensive way than he ever could when he walked its roads and climbed its hills.

The Resurrection was first *into* the universe, not out of it.

Because of what happened on Holy Saturday, the Christ who was raised on Easter Sunday was a Christ who now personified a restored Creation. The world, too, had been raised to glory when the stone was moved away. On Holy Saturday Jesus began transforming the body of the world into his own body, so that when the one body was established in glory, the other one was too.

I find a richness and a resonance in this way of reflecting on the unseen commerce of Holy Saturday's mystery. Nothing of the true faith is denied; and something deeper about it is clarified. It is also true to our mystical theologies of the Incarnation. It satisfies our soul in a way that the notion of Jesus ascending into heaven on his own, so to speak, leaving this world below him, doesn't. It contains the image of heaven breaking forth in great joy from the dark womb of the earth itself – but only because Jesus, with his wounds still raw, had first descended into that dark womb.

'Down into death he has penetrated,' wrote Karl Rahner, 'He let himself be overcome by death so that death would gulp him down into the innermost depths of the world. In this way, having descended to the very womb of the earth, to the radical unity of the world, he could give the earth his divine life forever. In death his sacred heart has become the pulse of the innermost heart of the world. And down here, the earth, in her continual development in space and time, sinks her roots into the power of all-mighty God. Now, it is an earth that is transfigured, an earth that is set free, that is untwisted, that is forever redeemed from death and futility.'

After all that happened beneath the deceptive silence of the first Holy Saturday, some theologians see the Resurrection on the following day in the image of the first eruption of a volcano which reveals God's fire now burning in the innermost bowels of the earth. Jesus' Resurrection was a real and cosmic rhythm of glory, dancing out the good news that this new world had already started turning, that the divine power of a transfigured earth was already leaping from the inner heart of the world – that world which Jesus had invaded to complete what his father had begun.

Holy Saturday's Divine Office recalls the most moving words of Jesus, having gate-crashed hell, to an astonished Adam and Eve, symbolising all humanity and all creation: 'In the past I threw you out of my garden; now I have come to take you home. Then I posted the cherubim to guard you as they would slaves; now I make the cherubim worship you as they would God.'

Alone on that long, misty, east-coast shoreline, I was moved and excited by such a beautiful theology of redemption. It ties the heart of Jesus to the heart of the world. He, now, is the essence of this earthly world. That is why it is all right to love the world with all its terrible beauty. We do not need to leave the world to find heaven. God is always, already, at the heart of the world.

Many of us, shaped by a small theology, settle for the limited goal of a personal salvation. But the Holy Saturday story invites us to explore a bigger horizon. To know that Jesus has taken the fight into the realms of the world's prince of darkness itself, and there radically and forever redeemed and restored its original beauty – that is a timely truth for a fear-filled world. Both the terrorists among us and those within us have been identified, encountered and transformed. Jesus has left no loophole unrepaired, for any new evil to steal in. In spite of all that would deny its validity, our Easter hope affirms and confirms the sacred civilisation of our world.

As I drove home it occurred to me that the Easter Vigil does not really end the hidden intensity of Holy Saturday. There is a sense in which it is always Holy Saturday. And it will continue to be Holy Saturday until the last day; until that day when this world ends in the universal Easter Sunday. It has to be this way. It is always Holy Saturday whenever people push back the creeping boundaries of the world's fear, making room for irrepressible hope; where people live the long darkness of original sin while believing in the possibility of the deeper light; where people discover the touch of an invincible spring on the bare branches of their winter lives.

Today we are free to imagine the Risen Christ, triumphantly bursting forth from the haunts of Hades, holding tightly the whole world to his breast with the great and jealous love of a mother for her child, nursing, nourishing and restoring it to its original unity in the heart of God. Small wonder our glimpse of suns that spin and dance on homeland hills each Easter Sunday morning.

Protected by an Embrace

God is as accessible as our next chat over a cup of coffee

It happened in May last year. Easter was well and truly over and Pentecost was beckoning. Tired after Monday's disappointing golf, I checked the answerphone. It was a woman's voice. 'Sir, I would like to have my baby christened next Sunday.' I tensed. She didn't even know my name. Neither was she aware of our 'two months' notice' requirement. Or the need for the prebaptismal talks. I fumed like this for a while before ringing back. 'Look,' I said, 'it's not as easy as you think. Can you come round next week so I can fill you in on a few matters?' 'No,' she replied, 'you'd better come round here!'

I did. I came to her house with my shield and spear at the ready. I was in indignant mode. After all, rules are rules. There are diocesan regulations to be honoured; we cannot just go around, as we used to, baptising everything that moved. It is due to such mistakes in the past that only a fraction of Catholics practise their faith now.

The young mother's face was discoloured. She told me that she was just out of hospital after a bad beating at the hands of her boyfriend. There was a sadness in her voice. Looking into the small cot with great love, and a sudden smile, she said, 'I do not want what happened to me, ever to happen to my baby. I feel she would be safe with your people.'

We talked for a while. My heart melted. I promised to do what she wanted, to make it all as easy as possible for her, to protect her little daughter from whatever threatened her fragile presence in a precarious world.

Another priest told me a similar story. When he, also slightly affronted by a brusque phone call, went round to the house, the mother explained to him that she had fought tooth and nail to bring her child to full term, in spite of the pressures and threats of her boyfriend, and even of her own Catholic family, to have an abortion. We both compared notes about how suddenly our approaches had changed. How ashamed we felt at our self-righteousness and ego-hurt. How far we had drifted from the compassion of Jesus! Such experiences in my life have led me to try a different way of looking at our role as pastoral, non-judgemental servants of God's people.

Are we still placing burdens on their shoulders? Are we still expecting them to dance to our tune, to jump through all kinds of ecclesiastical hoops before they can be worthy of joining us? Our parish preparation programmes are, of course, good and necessary. But they are only one way into the family. John Shea suggests that Jesus was crucified because 'he made God as accessible as the village well'.

Towards the end of the celebration of baptism one of the ritual prayers has an ambiguous phrase, 'Now you are a child of God.' Every Sunday I explain to the adults its true meaning. From the very first moment of its life, and long before it is brought to church, the baby is already made in God's image. 'Here comes God again!' the mystics would exclaim at the arrival of every new baby.

Maybe there is never another time in its life when it is closer to its Creator than now. And maybe the whole point of baptism is to keep it that way; to protect the little one not just from its own potential for sinning, but also from 'the sin of the world' that is waiting to destroy its lovely soul.

I reflected much on that young mother's remark the day I called to talk about a baptism for her precious baby. There was a pleading in her eyes as she said, 'I feel she would be safe with your people.' Maybe she had got it right and that this is the true theology of baptism. Maybe the baby is in reasonably good shape on arrival, but then the people of Jesus gather round it to keep it safe from the unfriendly fire of a world that can no longer distinguish enemy from friend, to be purified and nourished and kept safe from the smallness and closedness we call 'original sin'.

Baptism is such an exciting sacrament. It is about one of the most intimate moments in a family's life, and yet it has, too, the cosmic reverberations of the universal implications of the first Easter. The finest and most elemental symbols in the world are used with abandon, and the words and titles addressed to the child are spilling over with almost unbelievable wonder and delight. Not so long ago, just as my thumb touched the newborn's forehead to 'claim her for Christ', the most beautiful smile spread across her sleepy features. It seemed to me as though that little heart was rejoicing for having found the completion it came to search for!

Here is the magic of God in the magic of a baby. Here is infinite power in the vulnerability of a small child. Here is the divine essence in the dynamic fragility of a tiny frame. Baptism is Christmas, Passover and Pentecost rolled into one. This kind of ritual lifts us into another realm of being. It turns the world on its head. A dribbling baby is designated as the temple of the Holy Spirit. A very defenceless human being, who can neither read nor talk, is called a divine priestess, a prophetess and a princess.

The earthiness of the incarnation is in the celebration of baptism. The smearing with oil is sensuous and perfumed; the baby is wrapped in the white garment of God's love like the warm towel after a bath near the fire; the candle of light is the comforting embrace when fear chills our body and soul. And the truth of water, that old mother from whose womb we once emerged, is still our guarantee of vibrant life.

I like to think of baptism as a kind of celebration of the senses. And I like to think of the senses as thresholds of the soul. There is a lovely moment in the baptismal ceremony when the priest touches the ear and mouth of the baby. He prays that she will never be destroyed by the poison of hate-filled talk. May the ears of her heart be ever allured by the music of God's present moment, with its songs and stories. Touching her mouth, he prays that she will never use her gift of speech for anything but spreading love, encouragement, forgiveness and joy. And this, after all, is more or less what that young mother in my opening story was asking for her baby.

A frightened child calls out to his mother during a night of nightmares. She rushes into his room and tries to comfort her crying son. 'There is no danger,' she reassures him, 'there are no ghosts or dragons here. You are well protected by your guardian angels and by my prayers. In fact, God is here to keep you safe.' The child will not be consoled. All her efforts were in vain. 'Can't you see,' he pleaded, 'I want something with skin on.' And, of course, that is why God took a human body.

Against an Infinite Horizon

Every human heart, religious or not, is on a universal pilgrimage to God

I'm alone for a moment, on the ferry home, half-way between Calais and Dover. It is Sunday morning and the sun is shining on the green-blue sea. As spring turns to summer, millions travel to Lourdes. Our own parish pilgrimage is almost over. Our hearts are full of stories of pain and joy, of some dark moments and many bright ones, of shared secrets, and glimpses of the mystery and paradox of the human spirit.

And now that those famous white cliffs are coming into view, Dorothy, one of our doctors, joins me for a chat. Very apologetically, and trustingly, she admits to having some difficulty in 'buying into' the legend of Lourdes, not to mention its commercial and materialistic trappings. I cannot say that I'm shocked at hearing this. There is, I feel sure, a doubting Thomas lurking in all of us. Our finest saints were racked by doubts for long, empty years. Even Jesus himself, on the cross, may have died in a lonely winter of the spirit.

Whether we travel to Lourdes, then, to relieve the pain of those less able, as Dorothy did, or because we ourselves are desperate for healing, as I was, our nagging questions can draw us into deeper truth. It is possible to be part of the mystery of Lourdes at a very fundamental level of experience. Because our human condition is never complete, there is, deep in our souls, a yearning for wholeness. From all time, and in all cultures and religions, people carry within them a searching for the transcendent, a quest for God, like an unfinished symphony.

From the very beginning, people on pilgrimage carry lighted candles and other symbols of enduring hope, like we did, at the Torchlight and Blessed Sacrament processions; they bathe in water like we did at the Baths, or bless themselves, like we did, with drops from the green river; they touch the rocks of Mother Earth as we did at the Cave; they sing and chant familiar refrains, like we did to the rhythm of the Rosary; they take off their shoes when they are on holy ground like we did, to have our tired feet anointed; they kiss the icons and images of their salvation like we did, and like our departed Pope did, during his many visits to his beloved Lourdes, when he knelt down to kiss the dust of the world's pilgrims – the dust from which we came and to which we will all return.

At Lourdes they tell stories of how, one day, God's mother appeared to a country girl, and of how the lives of visitors, for a century and a half, have been changed for ever. Each religion of the world has its own version of this story. Deep down, we all sense a belonging in that universal human journey. Every morning and evening, as we found our place in that winding, evocative procession of light, we sensed our solidarity with the innumerable pilgrimages of people around the world, journeying through existential darkness, trusting in the power of their own deities, and of their own holy lights, to guide them safely to their destination.

Lourdes is not the place for proofs and certainties. It is foolish to be too dogmatic when dealing with mystery. We are best advised, when approaching the unknown, to do so on our knees. Enough to know that our own personal stories are held within the greater story of God. With our sisters and brothers across the nations, we, at the foot of the Pyrenees, felt humble, vulnerable and grateful.

And maybe that is why, at our daily times of sharing, some shy paradoxes emerged. We, the giving helpers, began to realise that, truly, we were the receivers, too. The roles were somehow reversed. Even though we, the able-bodied, were the ones who walked behind the wheelchairs of our physically less able sisters and brothers, we were the emotionally disabled ones who so desperately needed healing through the love and acceptance of our 'guests'. Within our group there were many stories told of such 'small revelations'. Beyond the limitations of denominations, Lourdes, we agreed, is not the place for wearing masks.

Perhaps then, among its many other graces, Lourdes can be experienced as an opportunity and an invitation to join our sisters and brothers of the world over, in the journey of their souls, in the rituals of death and life, of despair and hope, of pain and joy, especially when we gathered around the universal elements of bread and wine.

Lourdes is the world in microcosm, the church in miniature. All of life is there. It is open to all who are searching for meaning, for healing, for wholeness. It asks for no spiritual passport, no certificate of worthiness, no official invitation. If you are hungry, the table is set just for you. If your wounded heart is open, it will be healed. Beyond historical facts and fictions, beyond proofs and doubts, beyond disposable kitsch and artistic treasures, one can hear at Lourdes – and at all the sacred places of divine incarnations across our planet – the voice of a passionate God saying, 'Because I love you so much, I only want to heal you.'

At Lourdes, that metropolis of teeming and intense emotion, everything is turned around. It is a place of divine contradiction, of ultimate questions. Who are the valuable members of our society? What are its core values? Are we all driven by unworthy motives? What, or who, will bring us to our senses – before it is too late? The essence of Lourdes is a humbling experience for many of us. We begin again to realise that we cannot control God, or fashion God to our own specifications. God, by definition, is always different, always bigger than our creeds and churches. In his *Orthodoxy*, G. K. Chesterton wrote about the Catholic ability to hold opposites, doubts and contradictions together. Mystery and tradition are big enough to cope with conflict and paradox. The reasons for our hope are not based on a defined certainty, but on a huge trust in, and respect for, divine freedom.

There is a sense in which God's healing, then, can never be confined to one story, one place or one moment. No one belief system holds the monopoly of divine compassion. There will always be a wild extravagance about God's amazing obsession with us. In Faber's beloved hymn (1855), we remember that 'There's a wideness in God's mercy/Like the wideness of the sea.'

For the Christian, a miraculous light shone over Bethlehem. It shines on, especially in the marvellous events that happen at Lourdes. But for millions of this planet's pilgrims, the miracles of our great and saving God are not confined to any one place. Against the infinite horizon of a totally free and utterly unlimited Lover, against a sky of a million bright lights, the Christian star finds its true and perfect setting.

Home's a Holy Place
Whether in ecstasy or agony, married life remains an epiphany of God

My brother Joseph had Down's syndrome. Every so often, in my dreams, he still comes storming back to deeply disturb my life. My mother adored him. And during those most difficult times, especially when Joseph's severe diabetes demanded unrelenting attention, she was sustained by the certainty that in caring for Joseph she was entertaining angels unaware. If I had my mother back now I would tell her that it was even more than that. It was the Lord himself who was there.

The same is true for every member of every family. Even today, when the notion of 'family' is undergoing radical change, it is still true. The mystics believed that God is born anew in every child. 'Here comes God again', they would say, 'in deep disguise. The seed of God becomes God. Just as the pear seed becomes the pear tree, and the hazel seed becomes the hazel, so too, God's seed in us becomes God.'

And all of this happens in the living rooms and kitchens of every family. The home is, indeed, a holy place. It is the nursery of divinity. And, as with our Joseph, and all those who are different, it can be a long nursery with no graduation day. As midwives of mystery, the work of many parents is unrelenting. Their whole lives are spent in persuading and coaxing, with the mother-tongue, God's incarnate, unfamiliar beauty from within reluctant shadows into the light of day.

When parents are gathered on Judgement Day, the Lord will gently say: 'I was hungry and you fed me, thirsty and you gave me a drink, naked and you clothed me, homeless and you sheltered me, imprisoned and you visited me. Come; enter the kingdom I have prepared for you.' And the parents will be bewildered and ask: 'Are you sure, Lord? When did we see you hungry and feed you?'

The Lord will reply, 'Do you really not know? Do you not remember the way you carefully fed me when I was a baby; the way you loved me into my first small steps across the kitchen into your arms, and later, my bigger steps into the waiting world? All the time, that was me you were nourishing. Yes, of course it was your child. But it was me, your God, as well.'

'When were you thirsty, Lord?' they asked. 'I needed your love and comfort. You held me to your breast and I could hear your heart. As tenderly as the sun opens the daisies in the morning, your gentle voice and loving eyes opened my soul to the mystery of my true identity. I, your God, became your vulnerable child so as to experience your tenderness to me.' 'But naked, Lord? And homeless?' The Lord replied, 'I was born naked and homeless, and you sheltered me, first in your womb and then in your arms. In my rebellious years I left home, blinded by lesser lights and loves. You did not judge me; your great heart never doubted me; you forgave me, you believed in me, you drew me into a higher way of life-making, light-making and love-making. No matter what, on my return home, your face at the door was always a smiling sacrament of welcome.'

'But imprisoned, Lord? Surely not!' The Lord paused. 'There are many kinds of prison. When I was imprisoned in my fears I cried out in the night; you came and lifted me from behind the bars of my cot and folded me in your arms. Years later you lifted me from behind the bars of bigger fears – fears of my own inadequacy, of my own intense emotions, of the terror and beauty of the unknown life ahead.'

Perhaps nowhere more than in the heartfelt dynamic of married life, where the human spirit stretches itself, in its trusting and letting go, to the limits of its potential, is this expression of incarnate love more clearly sacramentalised. We discover that every ordinary human home is the unexpected place where God dwells. Even where there is suspicion and deceit, married life must remain an epiphany of mystery; a participation in God's own challenging essence. Anytime we say, 'I'm trying to forgive you' or 'I still believe in you' to each other, that is also the ever-present expression of God's incarnate covenant within us, constantly healing and completing all that is imperfect.

Holy Week teaches us that we can only experience the Risen Christ when we have undergone some kind of loss or disillusionment. Most of these 'little deaths', and the more awful ones, too, are found within the world of the home. Because of its potential for creating joy, family life can also be a den of destruction.

Where is the divine heart in the way we crush the life out of each other behind closed doors? And yet, is not the very hopelessness of our lives the only place for hope to happen? Where else, if not in this loveless noise, and against all the odds, can the faint music of Easter be recognised within us?

There is an urgent energy within our domestic world waiting to be released into the church. The home is a cauldron of emotions, all now charged with redemptive presence; for that reason it is also a powerhouse of renewal within the church. The passions and prayers, the storms and whispers, the blame and the blessing – are all part of that graced energy. Everything that happens in the unbelievably complex fabric of family life, the light and the dark of it, has God's life-giving heartbeat within it, God's loving signature set to it. And we go to Mass to remember and to celebrate together the extraordinary revelation that no moment is 'merely' human or worldly, but rather a place of grace; every threshold a door to heaven.

With this vital 'secret' in mind, we insisted on designing a welcoming living room into the foyer of the lovely new church we built a few years ago. In this hearth, people sit around the open fire, tell stories, read poetry, or chat. And each day, too, the same sacramental space is used for celebrating the Eucharist; nature and grace again embrace on the one small kitchen table of life. We placed these words on the mantelpiece so as to always remember:

Smiling broadly with great delight, Jesus, our only true host, sets a place for absolutely everyone at this table. He embraces every family, each with its own stories to tell him – the hurting and the healing, the sinning and the gracing. He then sits down and explains to us, amazed, how those ordinary moments of raw human life are his life too. His eyes are twinkling as we struggle to understand what he is telling us. Comforted, we eat and drink his words with the bread and wine of joy. He kisses each one of us before we leave. Our hearts are burning within us as we recall his parting words of comfort – our kitchens, too, are little Bethlehems, our breakfast tables are small altars, our whole lives, with their calvaries and resurrections, are one long consecration and communion. But now we are so slow to leave him. 'Don't be sad,' he says, 'I'll be waiting for you at home.'

Anger of a Struggling Heart
When clerical masks fall and human tears flow

I could feel the anger coming on. If he does not stop soon, I was thinking, I'm going to lose it. He didn't and I did. With little warning, the red mist struck.

It does not happen to me very often. I can count on one hand the number of times that I've exploded in company. Strangely enough, I haven't ever regretted those out-of-control moments. There was always something real about them. When such outbursts happened I have felt the hard thrill of truth, the brief satisfaction of being myself, the strange comfort of expressing my own real, though flawed, humanity.

As with many who are in the public eye, so much of my life, too, as a parish priest is about masks. The all-pervading clerical role so often takes over my human face. There is a constant struggle going on inside me. There are times when the expectations of others, of my early upbringing and of my own fearful obedience, almost suffocate my soul. Yet in each of those unexpected exchanges, when my normal self-control breaks down, I have felt a release, as though liberated, for a moment, from some strait-jacket of conformity.

Like many other colleagues, in the course of our work, I fume inwardly. Too often, I'm conscious of an inner seething, a slow-burning resentment that is usually held firmly in check. This constant emotional control is costly in terms of good energy and overall health. At such times I can almost feel my arteries thickening, my hair whitening and the crow's-feet deepening around eyes and mouth.

But does it have to be this way for us priests, I often wonder? How many of our married parishioners are diminished by these debilitating tensions and passing encounters? I am well aware that marriage is not always a bed of roses. But is there a difference when it comes to coping with the kind of emotional moments I'm writing about? Does the wound, small though it may be in light of the huge suffering of the world, heal more quickly when it is shared with a partner?

Supposing I come home from chairing a meeting where I'm harshly criticised or challenged. I'm feeling sorry for myself, hard done by and unfairly treated. With or without justification, I'm hurting. To be able to share this bit of pain with my partner, and to hear her say something like 'Oh, forget it; everyone knows what Bernard is like!' or 'I shouldn't worry about that remark. Susan says it to every new parish priest.' How helpful and releasing would that be. Or have I got it all wrong? Do husbands and wives not talk like that to each other?

Even though we often present ourselves to our parishioners as confident, competent and self-sufficient men, if truth be known, we are, when alone at night, in our often vast presbyteries, pathetically insecure. Without the comforting voice, touch, listening ear of another, we so easily magnify the ordinary incident into a highly charged personal attack on our integrity or competence. Small wonder we often become awkward, neurotic, defensive or depressive. Without the normal, commonsense street savvy of my closest friends, I would continually tend to magnify the trivial put-down into a major disgrace. It is only when priests trust each other as human beings that they hesitantly admit to such quiet desperation.

As with appropriately expressed anger, there is a healing too in weeping. In my life I find they are connected. Without going into detail here, there is much disillusionment, a sense of loss, and a well-hidden anger within the walls of many a presbytery just now. There are many who will disagree – on the grounds that they themselves are in fine fettle and that the priesthood is in good shape in every way. And anyway, only wimps cry. This response, I feel, is part of the subtle grip of clericalism. I'm sure I speak for many silently struggling hearts.

Once or twice when I have cried in trusted company, the cause of the tears had to do with the relentless effort to conform, to be right, to avoid criticism, to please the parishioners on the one hand, the authorities on the other. So often I have longed to find and use my own voice, to speak my own truth, to tell it as I see it. Enforced loyalty to the party line is an exhausting demand that one day leads to a divided heart.

May I clarify something here. In my efforts to be authentic, to integrate the unpredictable dimensions of my life, to empty myself of unnecessary baggage so as to be of more use to others, I'm not recommending selfish or inappropriate behaviour. I'm simply pointing out that I've noticed some paradoxical kind of therapy around those times that I publicly lost my composure. I struggle when I try to put into words what precisely that 'inner healing' actually is. Perhaps it reveals what is really going on deep down within us; a moment of stopping pretending, of something authentic inside us shouting 'Enough is enough; I can't take it any more!' Better an external break-out than an internal breakdown. All I'm exploring here is the human need to express our emotions. Unfortunately, if this does not happen in a civilised way, it tends to burst out at the wrong time.

Not so long ago I 'lost it' during that sensitive time just before Mass – the time when celebrants are desperately trying to hold everything together. A queue of people had lined up with the usual requests – pray for Mary's exam, plug the special collection, and, of course, can you sign a Mass card before you begin? Then came the last straw. 'You forgot to mention my Grandma's anniversary last week, Father.' That did it. 'Your problem', I said, 'is that I'm not perfect. I'm a messed-up, forgetful, sinful person like everyone else.' How extraordinarily difficult it is then to walk out on to the sanctuary to celebrate the Eucharist, to preach the homily with a loving power, after an encounter such as that!

I am working on strategies to cope with such emergencies. As you can see, they do not always work! In a nutshell, when the trigger event happens, I remember to breathe consciously, mindfully. This is hugely important. It gives me enough space to create a tiny distance between the rising emotion and my rational response; enough room for the grace of choice. Beyond denial, fight or flight, I can now choose how I'm going to respond. And that is everything. I can transform the negative thing rather than transmit it. I can heal it rather than project it. That fleeting opportunity is a 'threshold moment'. It is Passover in miniature. Salvation in seconds.

I do enjoy my work. To be called, by God's power, to be a liberator of souls, a healer of wounded hearts, is a breathtaking ministry. But today, I'm simply revealing a little of my weaker side. I'm now discovering that the more vulnerable I become as a human person, the more authentic I am as a priest. The light and the shadow – they need each other always; they dance together to give the colour to our lives. As Rainer Maria Rilke said, 'If I manage to get rid of my demons, I fear my angels may leave as well.' The amazing mystery of our complex humanity is not always the easiest cross to carry, or the most comfortable crown to wear.

Memories on a Breeze
The heaven of childhood haunts and disturbs our hearts forever

Summer days and childhood memories! When they come together, they twist our hearts without warning. The remembered smells, sights, feel of summer so often strike, with painful intensity, at the tender, forgotten and sleeping magic of those special years. There is a pathos, a poignancy and the strangest sadness in those moments of memories 'that bless and burn', as my mother used to say.

This year I feel unusually vulnerable to the mixture of feelings within me as another summer blesses us, and as flashes of my childhood return. You may write it off as sentimentality but, in recent weeks, something within me opened up when I heard, within the space of one afternoon, Eva Cassidy singing *Fields of Gold*, Frank Sinatra's *The Summer Wind* and Val Doonican's *The Special Years*. It is never easy to put a name to the emotions that are stirred when that indelible and invisible grain of our tender psyche is touched again.

Another such occasion occurred recently at a small family reunion. Swaying bluebells were all over the wooded areas near the Yorkshire pub where my sister, my brother and I had a meal. Maybe because we were reminiscing about when we were small, a memory, or something deeper than a memory – more like a vivid, subliminal experience – came flooding back. When I saw those shy bluebells under the trees, I was instantly transported to another place – to Rathmore, in the south west of Ireland. At that moment I could remember exactly where I was standing, over 60 years ago! It was near St Joseph's convent, across the road from our little shop. I was barefoot. There was an afternoon sun slanting down the roof of the church. My mother was standing talking to a neighbour in front of our small shop window. They were leaning on some makeshift metal bars that my father had erected to protect the glass from the shoppers' bicycles, often thrown carelessly against it. (What they usually wanted, on their way home from a long shift at the new Fry-Cadbury's chocolate factory, was a packet of Sweet Aftons and a copy of the weekly *Kerryman*.) I was closing the green gate with the awkward, rusty handle. My sister and I were holding bunches of bluebells that we had picked in 'the nuns' field', for Our Lady's altar. I remember thinking, 'They're looking at us, they're smiling at us and they're talking about us.' Is it the light that makes a moment unforgettable?

I mentioned that I was barefoot. We used to shed our shoes on the first warm day in May. There is a timeless thrill that fills me when I remember, and almost physically experience again, that first day of summer when we 'went barefoot'. To feel the warm texture of the road tar, the dry sensation of the little wooden bridge, the coolness of the stone flag outside our door, the soft, wet grass, the sharp gravel, the oozing mud between our toes in the shallow stream that ran through the four green fields behind our house! How is it that my memories of touch are stronger through my feet than through my hands? Strong and gentle as the touch of the human hand is, maybe there is a sensitivity in our feet that carries the more lasting memory.

But back to our mini-family reunion. As we were saying our goodbyes, we noticed a hawthorn bush and a lavender tree growing in the car park. In the soft air of that Sunday afternoon, their aroma was strong. 'Do you remember John Sullivan's field?' my brother asked, as we inhaled the smells that stirred the memories of our hearts. Not only did we remember that sloping field, but, in a moment of pure gift, we were transported back there – and back to all the fields of our childhood. It was as though that particular experience, brought on now by breathing in the scent-filled air, had lain untouched and undiminished within us. Maybe this is what Gerard Manley Hopkins meant when he wrote about 'The deepest freshness deep down things'.

Once or twice during this May and June, as though suddenly released from captivity, all kinds of forces have rushed into my consciousness – bright and vivid images from the distant past. (There are, to be sure, winter ones too. But for now, let me stay with summer.) I keep recalling a poem I have always loved. *Fern Hill* by Dylan Thomas still brings an elusive poignancy to my whole being. It allows me to remember with gratitude the times I revelled in being young and new, especially during one long summer morning of childhood:

... it was all shining: it was Adam and maiden.
The sky gathered again
And the sun grew round that very day.
So it must have been after the birth of
the simple light in the first spinning place ...

Before she died, I used to ask my mother what was I like when I was small. She invariably said that I was always full of joy, wanting to celebrate everything, forever looking for reasons to break the routine of things. She said my world was a playground. I was a hero; I was a rebel – and I was full of wonder. Much too slowly, each dawn arrived, wrapped in another mystery, another adventure. My every breath, she smiled, was drawn in excitement.

Now as I was young and easy under the apple boughs
about the lilting house and happy as the grass was green;
the night above the dingle starry;
time let me hail and climb
golden in the heydays of his eyes.

My mother said I was always laughing. And always dreaming. And always wanting more than my head or heart or arms could hold. Effortlessly I moved between the real and the really real. Looking back now, I must have been living in some kind of sacramental world. Everything was now, and everything was forever.

And honoured among wagons, I was prince of the apple
towns,
and once below a time I lordly had the trees and leaves
trail with daisies and barley down the rivers of the windfall
light.

My mother also believed that I was one with nature then. I clung to the high branches of the swaying trees when the Atlantic summer winds blew magic around our house in the Valley of the Rushes. There was music everywhere for my bare and dancing feet. There was a green bough in my heart and the singing bird came to it every day. As Jesus himself said, this must surely be what heaven is about.

But, I sometimes wonder now, what if that green bough withers? What if that childhood laugh and dance and music

71

grows too silent, too soon, within us? What if the bluebells no longer send us catapulting inward to our magic places? This is what worried the farmer-poet Patrick Kavanagh when he felt that his adult sophistication had muted the distant drumbeats that still echoed somewhere inside him.

Sour is he as spinster's mouth
At kissing-time or time of praise;
His well of gladness dry, the drought
Of desert knowledge is his days.
O child of laughter, I will go
The meadow ways with you, and there
We'll find much brighter stars than know
Old Aldebaran or the Bear.

Touch of the Divine

There is a raw and physical reality about a God who became human flesh

There is no sound like the fall of the earth on the coffin. It was the funeral of the mother of a priest-friend in Ireland. He had been so strong all that November day – at the Requiem Mass and in receiving the condolences of neighbours. 'Sorry for your trouble, Fr Dermot.' He was staring at the grave, his face hollow with loss. It was getting dark when his friend arrived from England at the cemetery. She simply placed her arm across his shivering shoulders. Immediately he yelled something out – it sounded like 'Why?' – and then, as in a sudden cloud-burst, he began to sob and sob.

I have often marvelled at the power of touch. How much emotion it releases, how much healing it brings. Any parent who has finally picked up their tired, tense and fractious children will know the soothing power of holding them closely to their breast. Skin has to be touched, arms are for holding. Sr Mary told me about the boy who rushed up to her in the playground claiming to have fallen and hurt his knee. After close inspection she suggested that he had made up the story. 'Well, Sister,' the disgruntled pupil muttered, 'couldn't you give it a rub anyway?'

There is a story about the fearful child who, during the night, called out for his mother. She came into his room and searched the dark wardrobe to put his mind at rest. He would not be consoled. She checked for lurking (small) monsters under the bed. All to no avail. She spoke to him about the protection of the angels and of the presence of God all around him. He still refused to be satisfied. Unknowingly echoing the deepest desire within all creation, he blurted out, 'I want something with skin on.'

When fragile people stand before us, leaden-eyed and hopeless, something tells us that the first thing that Jesus would have done is to hold them tenderly. Then, like Dermot, their taut bodies would relax, their breathing change and their tears begin to flow. Every day I notice faces that ache to be touched. As people come with heavy hearts for a healing conversation or Confession,

I think about the last time that the anxious edges around their mouths and eyes were traced by a loving hand. Maybe never since childhood. At our 'anointing meditations' many people cannot remember a time when someone held their hands, or touched their feet, so gently.

We are designed to be looked at, to be held, to be enveloped with tenderness. Just as God, according to Celtic folklore, placed a healing for all human illnesses somewhere in the vast variety of creation, so, too, God has built into the miracle of our human-ity – mind, body and spirit – the assuaging of the open wounds that would otherwise stay bleeding. Divinised twice, first by birth and then by baptism, our bodies are thresholds of God's peace, embodying and setting free the invisible mystery of true compassion and hope. That is why God became flesh in the first place.

Five-year-old Mortakai hated school. Every day he would es-cape from his teachers and head for home. No amount of reason-ing, promising or threatening made any difference. His parents were desperate. As a last resort they brought the little lad to their rabbi. After looking at Mortakai lovingly until he quiet-ened down, the wise old rabbi picked him up and held him to his heart for a long time. Nothing was said. But something very important had happened. What words could not accomplish, a silent embrace did.

We celebrate sacraments to body forth the presence of God. There is more to God than monologue. All the sacraments are touching places. There is a depth and richness to ritual. Ritual is to our love of God what an embrace is to lovers. It can say and do what words cannot express. Bodies and sacraments go to-gether. 'Without body – without sacrament,' writes the Welsh poet and artist David Jones. 'Angels only – no sacrament. Beasts only – no sacrament.' Without human flesh God would have re-mained for ever out of touch and out of reach. It would all be an angelic existence without substance, without salvation. There would be no real heart in it (1 John 1: 1-4).

Jesus lived fully in his body. He embraced young and old, placing his hands on sinners, offering no resistance to the head of John on his breast or to the sensation of Mary's hair on his naked feet. When he reached for his special friends in the most human of ways and yearned, as we all do, for intimacy, he was enfleshing and revealing the true nature of God incarnate. And for children, to be lifted up on to the back, or shoulders, or hips of Jesus was to be playing with God; to be hugged and kissed by him was to be hugged and kissed by God. The tempo of his heart was always in time and tune with the divine rhythm. Incredibly, it is the same with us (John 14:12). Incarnation reveals that the many expressions of human love are pulsing with God's love too.

'Our love is the work of God within the human heart.' As Pope Benedict expresses so clearly in *Deus Caritas Est*, human love is brought to completion in the love of God. And it can never be truly incarnated into our lives without rejoicing in the essential sacredness of the human heart in the human body. In his life, death and resurrection Jesus went far beyond words. So did God in creating humanity. And so does the Eucharist, when we actually eat the flesh of God and drink God's blood.

To be writing this reflection between the feasts of the Flesh and Blood of the Son of Man, Corpus Christi celebrated on Thursday this week, and the Sacred Heart of the Human One, to be celebrated next Friday, is a great joy. Both celebrations, so physical, so intimate, so universal and so incarnational, are given to us to remind us of these wonderful truths. At Mass, the body of the man Jesus is transformed into our bodies, and ours into his. We feel the flow of his wine-blood within, merging with our very being at a profound level of mutual surrender and transformation. The divine heartbeat becomes the energy that pulses in ours. Next Friday is the feast of all our sacred, human hearts.

Those precious moments after Holy Communion are marvellous in their sensibility. They have an immediate sensuousness and an experiential truth that can take our breath away. In one of his weekly homilies Pope John Paul II described our need of God in the Eucharist 'as physical as the need for food or water'; our desire for intimacy with God as 'instinctive and physical'. It is not by chance, he said, that the psalmist spoke of 'an embrace, of a clinging that is almost physical'. The Eucharist is God with skin on; it is God's hug.

Like Mortakai and his rabbi, God picks us up and holds us closely until we stop crying and our restless hearts find peace again.

At the Heart of our Lives

Skin needs to be touched. At Mass God holds us until we stop crying

'Rome Slams Abuses of the Mass'. Priests and parishioners are worried at these loud and recent messages about rubrical correctness around the sanctuary. Many objective commentators describe such Vatican warnings as sadly missing the point. Those who stop coming to Mass claim that they are bored by the irrelevance of our liturgies and homilies. The real issues, they say, are about what happens in their daily lives, and how the Eucharist might support and nourish them in their often desperate struggles.

So how do we set this beautiful sacrament free of all that would diminish it? How do we provide fresh, sweet water for thirsty people? And where do we begin?

I remember a story about an American football coach called Guy Lombardi. His team had plummeted from the top of the league. The previous season they had dazzled the country with the magic and sophistication of their passing strategies and scoring techniques. Now they had lost the plot completely. He called them together and settled them down. 'Let us begin at the beginning. This', he explained, 'is a football. And these', he said, 'are your legs and arms. Now the aim is to get that ball, using your legs and arms, from one side of the field to the other.'

Where do we find a simple but profound strategy for bringing the Mass to life? How do we reveal new depths to its mystery? A deeper understanding is reached, I feel sure, when we connect what we do around the altar with what we are doing each day of our lives. We celebrate the Eucharist so as to never forget its implications for our ordinary routines and chores. I see the Mass as the 'colouring in' of the pale outlines of the lives we bring to it. I see it as revealing the true worth of all that is going on within us and around us – disclosing and celebrating the hidden presence of God in the midst of the most common things.

Put more poetically, I like to feel that the bits and pieces of each day's jigsaw puzzle are put together at the altar; that the separate, often discordant notes of each day's living are fused into one flowing Sunday symphony; that the hurts, fears and shame of our lives are all held and embraced in this weekly ritual of bread and wine; that the Eucharist creates stories and poems out of the mixed-up alphabet of what happens to us each day; that, on Sunday, the scattered and broken beads of our fragmented existence are again refashioned into a necklace of pearls; that at Mass, we are astonished by the nearness of God who comes to us disguised as our lives.

Many dedicated pastors will want the people to feel affirmed at Mass, to be more aware of the holiness of even the most menial part of their lives, to appreciate the beauty and power they carry, to see the stumbling blocks of ill-health, breakdowns in relationships, anxiety over money, as potential stepping stones to a new life.

On a Sunday morning, I long for our parishioners to walk out of our church with a new spring in their step, a new look of confidence in their eyes, a holy determination to start all over again. I see them sitting there, pervaded by a strange and often heartwrenching innocence. There is loss in their faces, hope and delight, too, apprehension and guilt. I remember Marie's intense loss when her baby was stillborn, Eleanor's joy at achieving her A-level hopes, the shock of Harry when his wife walked out. 'You are all heroes and heroines exactly as you are,' I say to them. 'If you only knew how unconditionally you are loved, how cherished you are, how safe you are. Today's Eucharist guarantees that everything in your life is sacred. That nothing is lost. That no bitter tear or heartfelt wish is ever wasted. That no sin is ever left unredeemed. That everything, in the end, is harvest.'

Full of these thoughts I carefully hold the bread and wine. They are the fruit of the earth and work of human hands, symbols of the history of Mother Earth, signs of the often tumultuous struggles that rage within the human hearts of our congregation. Then, with all the graced intensity granted to me, I utter, over all of this astounding reality, the shattering words of God, 'This is my body: this is my blood.' Nothing is 'merely' human any more. Everything is now revealed as divinely human, shining with God's incarnate light.

In these ways I try to transcend an overemphasis on the rubrics and liturgical niceties of the daily or weekly ritual. Life is incredibly raw and violent. Passions ignite in a moment. Fierce emotions wage silent civil wars in the hidden places of our hearts. This is the raw material of our Sunday Mass. If it is not about our volatile, erratic and deeply powerful drives and emotions, then the Word has become flesh in vain. Where else can redemption happen if not at the point of our pain? From what else, other than the ever-present fear, jealousy, anger and despair, can we be saved? If the hard-won Eucharist of the Passover is to have any relevance to our lives, it must be felt at the very guts and marrow of our being, at those precarious places within us where our demons and angels meet. This is where our need is strong and urgent.

John Paul II describes this need of God's healing in the Eucharist as being 'as physical as the need for food or water'. He said that our desire for personal transformation is expressed in wanting an intimacy with God which is 'instinctive and physical'. 'It is not by chance', he says, 'that the psalmist speaks of an embrace, of a clinging that is almost physical.' I often ask our people to feel and reflect on the actual sacred and sensual awareness of the bread and wine within their bodies. Beyond words, this is another kind of life-giving intimacy.

Before he died, having exhausted what he could do with words, Jesus went beyond them. He gave us the Eucharist, his physical presence, his kiss, a ritual within which he holds us to his heart. Touch, not words, is what we often need. God has to pick us up, like a mother her child. Skin needs to be touched. Our bodies have their senses to be nourished. There are times when even holy words are not enough. That is why God became a baby, and why that baby grew up to become our Eucharist.

John Paul II's poetic and mystical soul delights in opening up all kinds of windows on to the richness of the mystery. In his most recent encyclical, *Ecclesia de Eucharistia*, he writes: 'I have been able to celebrate Mass in chapels built along mountain paths, on lakeshores and seacoasts; I have celebrated it on altars built on stadiums and in city squares. This varied scenario of celebrations of the Eucharist has given me a powerful experience of its universal and, so to speak, cosmic character. Yes, cosmic!

Because even when it is celebrated on the humble altar of a country church, the Eucharist is always, in some way, celebrated on the altar of the world. It unites heaven and earth. It embraces and permeates all creation. In the Eucharist, Christ gives back to the Creator and Father all creation redeemed.'

Resonating around the heavens, this magnificent and stirring vision of the Mass as the sacred song of praise for a wild and dancing cosmos, full of wild and dancing hearts, can never be contained in fearful and constricting regulations.

Everywhere in chains
The pathos of our trapped lives, yearning desperately for the light

There is a small red button on the crematorium lectern. When you press it, at the end of the service, the coffin slides through the curtains into the firechute. As I reached for the button, the doors at the back of the chapel suddenly swung open and a young, handcuffed man stumbled through. He was accompanied by two police officers – a man and a woman. The three of them came slowly, but determinedly, to the front.

The prisoner, Ben, allowed out for the occasion, was distraught. He tried to grasp both sides of the coffin as if to embrace his grandmother. In desperation he pulled violently, seemingly trying to smash the chains that were denying his hands and his heart. Finally he bent down and laid his cheek against the still-sticky, newly varnished casket and sobbed. The officers stood silent at either side, one impassive, one intense.

There was a rage in the young man's powerlessness. His frustration was tangible. He seemed impervious to the startled reactions of his family and relations. I wanted to walk over to him and hold him in that heartwrenching moment; to calm him at a time when words were worthless and only touch would heal. But I didn't have the confidence. I was too overawed, too overwhelmed by it all.

I had never witnessed anything like this before. The atmosphere was full of death and anger, of thwarted yearning, of desire and denial, of the strangest beauty in the middle of stark, raw emotion. If ever I experienced pathos, it was then and there.

Silently, another slight figure approached the small group at the coffin. It was the old woman's daughter, the young man's mother. Numbing grief and unbearable love filled her eyes. Gently, and with immense and graced authority, she put her arms around her manacled son. In a mutual kind of covenant, with a certainty and confidence beyond my understanding, she drew him to the nearest bench, near where I was standing. He lay across her lap, his limp body relaxed at last, his exhausted face on her shoulder, his dark hair lost against her black blouse. The police officers, aware of something beyond the normal, remained at a discreet distance.

A friend of mine was at the funeral. Like me, she was immediately locked into the unfolding drama, sensing something of the mystery of reality, of the interface between darkness and light, between death and life. As she watched that unforgettable scene of the mourning mother stroking and soothing her beloved son's head, an image of the Pietà came into her mind. The image and the moment have never left her.

As his two minders took Ben away to grieve alone, I was still shaken by the desperation of his efforts to express himself, to make contact with someone he adored, to break through into what was just beyond his reach. Another of Michelangelo's sculptures flashed before me. It was the carving of the 'emerging slaves'. Straining from the prison of their granite blocks, they were reaching for their freedom; confined in their darkness they were stretching, relentlessly, for the light.

The intensity of that image touches something in all of us. In the scripture reading at the funeral, St John reminded us that we are already the children of God, on the brink of blossoming into divine beauty. I am always filled with amazement at these words. I can scarcely believe what I'm reading. We are filled with the seeds, the glimpses, the echoes and the promise of the full possession of the divine essence. These real sentiments reverberate around the halls of our hearts. All of this is going to play havoc with our emotions and our grip on reality. We will, like Ben, be forever reaching beyond our grasp, drawn and driven by powerful forces within us.

Some of our best spiritual writers remind us that, because of the fathomless mystery of Incarnation, the energies and potential of God's own self are wrapped up within us now. This must be too much to hold together. How can the fragile, precarious human spirit contain the infinitely transforming and ultimately divinising power of God's enfleshed presence? Like atoms, we are waiting to explode. Like orphaned exiles of heaven, we are forever ready to risk escaping home. There is a loneliness and a secret need within us all that normal human intimacy will never completely satisfy. And there are times and places in our lives – mysterious moments – when such spiritual conflict is brought home to us with almost unbearable intensity. Ben's chained hands were hammering on the metal plate on the lid of the coffin that carried his grandmother's name. He was trying to break through confinement and impotence into another way of being.

Are we all tormented in somewhat the same way? If God has filled us with an insatiable yearning for life in its fullness, towards what is always over the horizon of our possibilities, then is it any wonder that we are tortured by the futility of our efforts to transcend our mortality?

Do any of us ever succeed in expressing our love fully? Do our childhood dreams and the hard reality of our adult lives ever even remotely touch each other? What kind of unspeakable loneliness, what inarticulate vision of fulfilment, would have, in the first place, driven that young man to drugs, theft and violence, to ruining his own life and that of his fiancée?

And as we reflected afterwards on that intense moment of human emotion, that brief disclosure of the pure passion of power and powerlessness, did we not all feel our own limitations? Did we not all somehow identify with the prisoner's rage, his inability to express the deepest desires of his heart just then, his frustrated outburst of despair? Were we not all battling with the chains around us, rattling the bars of our own cages, beating on the coffin of all that keeps us, too, captive?

The God within us is hungry for the light. The bright spark we were born with will forever burn close to the cold casket of death. We only fall into frustration when we mistake the pearl of true light for the transitory imitation of fool's gold. When the vision is lost, hope goes too. We do not need to stay hammering any more, like Ben, on the coffin of Good Friday. It is already open. We need no longer wait for the emerging slaves within us to escape the cold darkness. Once touched by the source of life, they can now run free, leaping and shouting, into the morning light.

The mystery of our humanity is only contained and given meaning once we set it against the bigger story of another reality, of a Risen Christ. In the Pietà image, Mary held, at once, the despair of her son's death, and the hope of his resurrection, within her arms. Her human heart, just then pulsing with intense grief and love, was able to transform and transcend the stark and dark reality that was enfolding her. Maybe this is what the grieving woman in the crematorium was able to do, too, when she touched the coffin of her dead mother with one hand and, with the other, drew her living son to her loving, trusting breast. And, in the shadow of last week's terrorist madness, maybe that is what we are all called to do – to hold wanton death and undying life in the one embrace – if we are ever to find hope in our darkest times.

Catching the Rhythm of Things

Our bodies resonate with the pulse of the earth. Nature is our spiritual guide

Relentlessly returning to re-gather along the horizon, *Tonn Clíodhna*, the white horses of the sea, in froth and fury, come driving fiercely towards me, only to vanish, like a breath, into the sand at my feet. This is the strand in Owenahincha, a tiny toe touching the warm skin of the Atlantic. To the east lies Inchadowney, to the north Reenascreena. Close your eyes and these place names will bring a smile to your face.

It is easy here, in this hidden haven on the south coast of Ireland, to swing and sway to the summer winds and to the rhythm of the sea. It is retreat time. I'm here with a group of people for whom the tension and intensity of their daily lives are almost too much. They are not alone. As we gather here in the last week of June, three newspaper articles have caught my eye.

The first informs us that one in three British men turn to drink to drown out their job stress, especially those working in the legal profession, in banking, medicine and education. Another, the government's recently published *Depression Report* by Professor Richard Layard, sets out a New Deal for restoring peace of mind to a nation in which one in six people (one in three families) suffers from chronic anxiety disorder. Just before that, the Department of Health's White Paper revealed that the second most popular service people wanted was one that brought mental happiness.

Reflecting here between our sessions, it occurs to me that too many of us are suffering from a new virus – the virus of alienation from our roots. Like swans on dry land, we are unsure and unsteady. We are no longer in our element. There is a deep disorientation because the compass that reveals to us our place in the grand scheme of things is out of true. We forget that we are part of a wider web. Dylan Thomas wrote:

The force that through the green fuse drives the flower
Drives my green age ...

The force that drives the water through the rocks
Drives my red blood.

All ground is holy ground. The land we stand on is sacred; we are connected to it and part of it. All we need, in our fretting and worrying, is to realise this truth, to be intensely aware of the connectedness of all things. It is in this connectedness to all things and creatures that we are connected to God. That is when we find a deep peace and freedom. It is only, as Sam Keen has written, when 'the moon rises in my blood, and suns are born and burst in the atoms of my substance, and I am one body with the world' that a profound joy fills the wells of my being.

Keeping those wells clear, clean and fresh is the work of contemplation – of stilling the disturbing thoughts, of staying free of the anxious images, of becoming quiet enough to find a whole new perspective on all that is going on in our lives. It is more like a dropping downwards, a sinking below the conscious waves of tumult, than a desperate conflict at the level of endless, mental arguments.

When we breathe into our restlessness and dis-ease, there is an immediate shift in our self-awareness. It can happen quite quickly. This is an experience of tangible grace: it is the inner place to which Jesus went when it all became too much for him. Jesus was forever trying to overcome his fear of his demons. Not all of us try so hard. We carry a fear of depth. Many would rather perish on the surface than explore the unknown within.

We are focusing here, during these long warm days of our summer retreat, on finding harmony within ourselves by falling in tune and time with the pulse of nature, of the sky and of the sea. This, we feel sure, is where the regaining of balance, of healing and of peace begins. It is the way of creation and incarnation. It is the way of sacrament. It is the way of the mystics. It is the way of God. Including, but transcending all hands-on remedies, therapies and medication for restoring our peace of mind, for mitigating the damage caused by pressure and stress, the basic rhythm of our lives holds the key to our overall well-being. Only connect. Otherwise there is no groundedness, rootedness or inner freedom.

To place oneself in the middle of what Rabindranath Tagore

calls the Stream of Life is to feel a new power and perspective, a healthy confidence and balance in the current of one's destiny, even with all its shadowy nooks and crannies, its alarming twists and turns, its many culs-de-sac and its roads less travelled.

> The same stream of life that runs through my veins night and day runs through the world and dances in rhythmic measures ...
> It is your same life that is rocked in the ocean-cradle of birth and of death, in ebb and flow.

Here in Owenahincha, whether feeling the spray of the ocean during the day or hearing its unique and muted murmur at night, we all felt an affinity with mystery. The sea and the soul are spiritual sisters. They call to each other. They need each other. The soul needs form and context. The sea needs to be named and experienced. This is why the spiritual is also physical – it spreads along the arteries of the embodied soul, through the seasons and turnings of the universe itself.

Moving to the tempo of the tides each morning, it was easy to visualise God's healing power touching our minds and caressing our troubled hearts. From our innermost centre where the Blessed Trinity lives, and from the mysterious love pressing on us from all around, all we had to do was to surrender to the truth of reality, to the embrace of the present moment, to the way things are. With practice it becomes easier, this experience of our essence, this sensing of the healing heartbeat of God in the silent pulse of our attentive presence – the rhythm of our breathing, the rhythm of our being, the rhythm of God. Leaving aside what Eckhart Tolle calls the 85 per cent of our thinking that contributes only to our fears, we discover another place of tranquillity inside us. Open to this overwhelming, but shy and subtle presence, this God-Being, an extraordinary sense of peace and confidence fills our soul.

In *Variation on a Theme by Rilke* Denise Levertov wrote:

> A certain day became a presence to me;
> there it was, confronting me – a sky, air, light;
> a being. And before it started to descend
> from the height of noon, it leaned over

and struck my shoulder as if with
the flat of a sword, granting me
honour and a task. The day's blow
rang out, or it was I, a bell awakened,
and what I heard was my whole self
saying and singing what it knew: I CAN.

The Infinity of Now

There is a divine horizon and vision around our most menial chores

A t eighty-four Samuel Beckett was asked about the possibility of his retirement. 'What!' he exclaimed, 'Me? Retire? Never – not with the fire in me now!' Not all of us are that lucky. In my travels I meet teachers and priests for whom the original vision of their vocation has all but disappeared. There seems to be a universal kind of *ennui*, a deep-seated sense of pressure, that is driving people to retire as soon as possible. Equally worrying, whether it has to do with increasing bureaucracy, target-setting or appraisals, the very soul seems to have dropped out of the world of work for many.

How do we restore a new energy to our lives by finding a lost balance and poise? Is there a way of building into our days a ground, a centre, and a reminder of what is at the heart of all our endeavours, something that would provide a context and a balance against which to measure and nurture our energies? An extraordinary thing is that it isn't really the amount of work we do that wears us out. Burn-out has more to do with the absence of enthusiasm and dedication. When we work with a passion, everything changes. When our heart is in our work, the work itself becomes a kind of extension of our hearts. Taking pride in what we do transforms the weariness.

Empty Monday faces behind wet windscreens
inching their grim way along the A64 into Leeds.
The work that awaited, was already destroying them.
And then I saw him, as I see him almost every day.
On the verge of the soulless carriageway, his face is beautiful with attention.
He is holding the details of his day against an infinite horizon.
Like a mother to her baby or a cellist to her instrument,
like a painter to his canvas or a priest to his altar,
the litter picker, with meticulous dedication, stoops carefully to renew the face of the earth.

When I go back to Ireland I'm always struck by the Angelus broadcast on television. It is a valiant effort to recover a kind of timing and fine-tuning of the way we are present to whatever we are doing at that moment. At twelve and at six, the bells are tolled. During the pealing, workers from a variety of professions are depicted as lifting their heads and pausing for the length of a few breaths.You sense they have shifted their awareness to another place. They have moved, for a moment, inside themselves, drawn to a horizon deep within their own soul. It does not seem to be so much a distraction as a way of living more fully in the present moment, of being more present and devoted to the immediate work of their hands and eyes.

I had a similar awareness when I joined the Benedictine monks at Pluscarden near Aberdeen for six weeks some years ago. The regularity of the relentless bells calling them from working to praying, and back again, was such a grounding habit. It felt as though both exercises were being connected; that their sources, in the deep centre of each monk's being, were now revealed as equal aspects of the same transcending presence. Thus graced and graceful, this 'physical mindfulness' would dissolve the edges between their work and their meditation, as they repeatedly recovered the rhythm and the seasons of their days and nights, their bodies and souls.

There is a story that I love which illustrates the grace of this awareness. Two men were building a wall – long and high, one at each end. When asked what he was doing, the first brickie replied that, for a start, he had no interest whatever in his work. A wall is a wall is a wall. He was bored and listless. Brick after brick, day after day, month after month. He longed for Fridays; he hated Mondays. With no interest or involvement, his work was slowly killing him.

'I'm creating a cathedral', murmured the other man. 'This is the South Wall of it. I've seen the plans. It will be such a beautiful building. I can't believe I'm part of it. When I watch the young children playing around here, I can see them and their own children, worshipping in this holy and lovely place for the decades of their lives.'

When talking to parents, teachers and priests, I often tell this story. It transforms the way we see things. It is what the

Incarnation has revealed. It is what the sacraments are for. It is why God created the world – so that we would one day tumble to the amazing reality that lies beneath what we too often term as 'ordinary'. That is why the story about the two workmen is called 'The Infinite Horizon'. There is an infinite horizon to every single, routine, menial task we perform. The heavens reverberate to the least of our whispers or acts of love.

The men in the monasteries lay down their tools and obediently and beautifully walk away from their fields, desks and benches, only so as to return to them filled with more reverence and wonder. St Benedict, for instance, kept reminding his cellarer to hold his pots and pans in the kitchen with the same respect and reverence as the chalices and ciboria are held at the altar.

The Angelus rings out over the countryside of Ireland, not to distract the people from their daily labour into a more heavenly reality. It rings out only so that the forgetful eyes of their souls can be reminded of the treasures of grace at their fingertips. As the Prophet said, beyond the boredom and pain, work has a divine dignity around it. It is love made visible. This is what the Eucharist accomplishes for us each Sunday. It parts the veils and reveals to us that the liturgy of the church serves only the liturgy of Life, that all work is holy work; that the sacred place we search for is the very ground on which we stand. That every bush is a burning bush.

In his book *Crossing the Unknown Sea*, David Whyte suggests that what opened the heart of Moses was not hearing God's voice from the bush saying 'You are standing on holy ground', but the moment he looked down and realised not only that he stood in God's presence, but that he had been standing in that presence all his life. Every step of his life had been on holy ground.

It is Moses in the desert, fallen to his knees before the lit bush.
It is the man throwing away his shoes,
as if to enter heaven and finding himself astonished,
opened at last, fallen in love with solid ground.

Whyte goes on to observe that the antidote to exhaustion is not necessarily rest. The antidote, he claims, is wholeheartedness. We often get so tired because of the gap between our true powers and the work we do, between the possibilities we sense and the opportunities we have. In other words we are not really present to what we are doing. 'You are only half here', he writes, 'and half here will kill you after a while.' He offers a delightful metaphor when he comments on a Rilke poem about the awkward way a swan walks until it is transformed once it sinks down into its element, allowing the flowing water to reveal the true harmony it always carried.

Our Precious Oasis

The small sabbaths we need to face the intense, urgent truth of our lives

Mr Casey was always courteous. He was the conductor on the bus that dropped me at Lisivigeen, near Killarney, for my first-ever summer holiday, eight miles from home. I was seven then. Our farmer friends were waiting at the crossroads. Mr Casey helped me down the three steps of the bus with my strapped and bulging suitcase. We waved him goodbye and set off across the fields for the farmhouse. No emperor ever rode more imperiously to his destiny in a golden chariot drawn by elegant thoroughbreds, to the music of the spheres, than I did, that August evening, in a bumpy old cart behind a farting old donkey.

The euphoric bubble quickly burst. As I unpacked my bag I discovered, to my horror, that I had forgotten the Chef Sauce. Let me explain. Chef Sauce was my life. Without it I could not eat anything. Our small shop, in those Second World War days, stocked a very limited supply just for me. In my mind I could see those two squat bottles with the smiling chef on the front, still standing on the shelf at home. Eight miles each way, this time on a bicycle, was a long way for my kind host to go to collect my golden nectar.

Intense efforts were made, some decades ago, to canonise a very holy and zealous missionary. His cause was scuttled when the Devil's Advocate (a prosecutor figure whose job is to prove the candidate unworthy of such a distinction – a role, incidentally, that was recently made redundant by Pope John Paul II) discovered that he had once written home, in some panic, from pagan territories, for the pipe (his Irish *dúidín*) which he had forgotten to pack. His undoing was tobacco – mine will be, when the time comes, Chef Sauce.

The memory of my first holiday reminds me of the universal need for some kind of 'sabbath time' in our lives: a time to withdraw from the relentless action of our routine commitments so as to understand better the nature of our daily treadmill; a stepping out of the parade so as to see it more clearly from a distance; a moment of difference in order to explore the sameness of the repetitions of our lives. Our new Pope has recently returned from a 17-day holiday of 'repose and reflection' in the Italian Alps. I like to think that the words vacation and sabbath carry the hope of our holy time (*kairos*) transforming what we do in ordinary time (*chronos*).

It seems to me, as a pastor, that many Catholics are defining a new shape for acceptable church practice. There is a growing *sensus fidelium* concerning the regularity of Mass attendance. Many now worship, not every Sunday, but maybe once every two or three Sundays. There is, however, a very sound reason for the church's insistence on weekly attendance. This time of worship can be seen as a precious oasis to flavour the rest of our week with the true spice of life; a breather to explore the love and meaning at the heart of all that we are and do; a small sabbath to reveal God's signature at the end of each page of our weekday pursuits.

The much-mentioned spiritual hunger of people today is not, I feel sure, for more religion or church activities. It is for contemplative space, for an inner freedom, for tastes and glimpses of their own elusive beauty. During a real vacation, a real sabbatical, we make room for dreaming, for rediscovering the kernel of our being, for playing safely with bare feet. If sin, in scripture, is about 'missing the mark' – something that happens when we follow misleading maps and unreliable compasses – then sabbath-time is for a lot of re-routing, for some fairly urgent U-turns and for finding a way out of the many newly discovered cul-de-sacs we have long been lost in.

In a *Tablet* article some years ago, the Benedictine Sister Joan Chittester pointed out that we have substituted more labour, hard play or work-out leisure for soulsearching and reflection, for intimacy and awareness. Our culture turns the sabbath into a race for escape, an opportunity for more addictions, a collection of distractions. We cannot stop to do much about anything. We do not stop at all in fact. We work every day of the week and pack even more into the weekend, using it to mop up what spills over from the working week. We take the children to play in the park while we sit in the car to finish writing a weekly or monthly report. The sabbath has become catch-up time instead of reflection-time. We have lost a sense of attention, of living in the present, of what the Buddhists call 'mindfulness'. No wonder we can come to the brink of human cloning and hardly notice it; that we can watch the oppression of half the human race and take it for granted; that we can allow our leaders to take us into an unjust and unnecessary war – one which we are already deeply regretting.

As well as holidays, Sundays and daily meditation-times, holy days of obligation are also meant to provide us with essential sabbath-time. These days were intended to be an opportunity for remembering a different life rhythm, for resisting the relentless drive to overwork, for arresting the way that our daily routine takes over. 'If you don't live your life, your life will live you.' Such days are important because they keep us focused on a reality, a way of being that includes, but transcends, the usual patterns of days and weeks. They take us back to our sources in God and remind us of our destiny in heaven. And, in between, they keep before us the comforting assurance that, whatever the mountains we have to climb, we are not alone, that our lives are permeated by the Holy Spirit.

Professor Eamon Duffy, in another *Tablet* article, railed against the powerful lobby that sought to abolish the few remaining holy days in the Catholic calendar. He admits that they are awkward and burdensome. They cause problems for the conscientious; they are ignored by the lax. But he sees them as among the few witnesses against the relentless dominance of the economic in our lives. In them, the ancient rhythm of the Christian liturgical year breaks through, interrupting our restless routines and thereby giving a deeper meaning to the often-shallow business of living.

The inconvenient demands of holy days of obligation – forcing us to rearrange our routines at some cost to conscience and pleasure – are not, in fact, outmoded restraints on our liberty. They are exactly the opposite. They are important reminders of our human dignity and freedom, signs of another and greater timetable, a remembering of those eternal values that we truly believe in, but which get repeatedly submerged beneath the torrents of relentless functionality.

I am anxious to clarify that there is nothing dualistic about the emphasis on sabbath-time. There is no inference that 'chronos' time is inferior to 'kairos' time. They are both endemic to the creative heart of God. But because, for all kinds of reasons – the main one being original sin – our gullible hearts are too easily led astray, there is a vital need for sabbath-time, or, if you prefer, Eucharist-time, to realise the hidden worth and infinite value in what we often regard as the most ordinary and boring dimensions of the lives we live. God comes to us disguised as weekdays.

Blessed are the Reconcilers

If we don't transform our hurts, we project them on to a cycle of negativity

Thousands of Catholics across the country will be preparing for the inevitable changes and challenges that September will bring to their parishes. Priests will be moved, parishes will be 'clustered' and radical church re-ordering will, no doubt, continue. All such breaking of familiar patterns usually brings emotional conflict.

At such times, like stars in a cloudy night, some special souls will nearly always emerge, bringing with them the light of sensitivity, healing and common sense. I call them 'special' because most of us, unthinking in our prejudices, myopic in our tunnel vision, rush in and take sides too soon. Not many can wait to discern and explore the bigger picture.

I offer these reflections during the month of August when, notionally anyway, there may be a few fleeting opportunities to prepare ourselves for the various challenges that may impact the context of our weekly worship. Not everyone is capable of playing the role of reconciler. Yet it is probably the most needed gift and service in the church and world today – whether in the context of a Lebanon war or a Niger famine, or of domestic or pastoral blood-letting. And it is only the compassionate soul, facing its own divisions, that can ever hope to make a difference where leaders and factions are driven by fixed certainties.

To be a reconciler is to be one of those who forever endeavour to flesh out in their complex lives the pattern of the dying and rising mystery of Good Friday and Easter Sunday. Instead of reacting to, resisting or reflecting back the negative emotions and attitudes of those around them, whether in a one-to-one, communal or wider context, they take into their own vulnerable spirit, like Jesus did, the arrogance, hardness and stubbornness of those they lead or serve or live with, their jealousies, cynicism and strange motives. This is costly, spiritual work. It is the occupation of the saint.

When I pray to be a reconciler I'm praying for the death of

my all-powerful ego. I'm praying for the grace to transform, within my own body and soul, within the most redeemed part of me, the sins into graces, the curses into blessings, the destructive forces into life-enhancing gifts. In our imitation of Christ the experience of redemption can come no better than this. So often, in our daily routine of getting hurt, what we usually do, either in selfjustifying anger or self-righteous brotherly or sisterly 'correction', is to add force to the negative energies, by turning them round and redirecting them with still greater velocity, in an even more subtly negative way, back to the source from which they came.

There is an extraordinary power in the manner in which the very physical presence of Jesus united opposites through the peace and love that encompassed him: 'In his own person he destroyed the hostility' (Ephesians 2: 16). Jesus had learned that if the small and unsatisfied ego is not transformed, then the negative emotions of envy, fear and hate will be either denied or projected elsewhere. We are indebted to the Franciscan priest Richard Rohr for the dictum: 'What we don't transform, we transmit.'

He describes the familiar process of both denying and projecting as 'scapegoating', from the Jewish ritual of putting your faults on a goat that was whipped out into the desert. We displace and project our negative emotions on to other people, other systems, by blame and outrage. It is so hard to carry the burden of our own flawed humanity. Only the true essence, not the ego, can cope with such anxiety, such ambiguity, such fragile insecurity.

If our pain is not transformed by reference to a wider horizon, to a regaining of true perspective, to a letting-in of God's vastness, it will always be transmitted to others. The destruction of mindless wars, global or local, can be traced back to closed and divided hearts.

Inner emptying and dying is so hard to do. Nothing outside us is transformed without the radical grace of inner conversion. The seemingly irreconcilable situations we encounter at home and in the community are but microcosms of a wider alienation. We live in a desperately destructive and divided world where evil is perpetrated under the guise of nationalism and religion. Very often there is no one to accuse or punish. There is often only the blind and trusting holding of human ignorance and pride, sin and failure, until our love and pain break through to resurrection. 'There is no redemptive violence,' writes Rohr, 'there is only redemptive suffering.'

In his *People of the Lie*, Scott Peck quotes an old battle-scarred priest who said, 'There are dozens of ways to deal with evil and several ways to conquer it. All of them are facets of the truth that the only ultimate way to conquer evil is to let it be smothered within a willing, loving human being. When it is absorbed there, like blood on a sponge or a spear into one's heart, it loses its power and goes no further.' Whenever a person, or a community, manages to achieve this heroic kind of ultimate sacrifice, then the whole world becomes a safer place to live in.

We always have a choice about making peace or war. I can choose to see the positive in the other point of view or I can decide to block it even before I have heard it. I can search for the negative in everything I hear or I can really try to understand better what I disagree with. I can keep trying to forgive those who oppose my plans at every turn, or become bitter about it. I can grimly choose to accept, to be a reluctant reconciler, even while I still hear whispers of revenge echoing along the narrow corridors of my heart. Even for Jesus there was no instant transformation. However, thank God, there are times too, when, discerning a sinister lack of peace in a clearly toxic environment, it is wiser to shake the dust of those people and places off our feet – and scamper, hopefully to return again when our spirit is stronger.

I find making the sign of the cross over my mind, body and heart to be a deeply reconciling little ritual. As you touch your forehead and chest, in the Eastern tradition you are opening the brow and heart *chakras* of vision and compassionate understanding. According to Jewish practice, as you touch your left and right shoulder, you are activating the spiritual centres of mercy (*chesed*) and strength (*geburah*). In the Christian tradition we open ourselves to the influence of the Blessed Trinity, to the creator and sustainer of the world, to the saviour and reconciler of its sins, to the healing spirit of new beginnings. In the end it is the cross alone that will hold the opposites together and transform them. And only the light will then be transmitted. When I bless myself, the world too is blessed.

Beauty and the Priest

We ache for beauty. For beauty we are created. It is the sacrament of God

It was a dark, eerie Friday afternoon at the end of March. The children were racing from our local school to the waiting bus. Suddenly a girl noticed the magnificent rainbow. There it was, an arc of beauty, elegant as a ballet dancer, stretching gracefully across the bloodshot sky of our small city. Fine-tuned as they were to the play of light and shade, to the dance of colours, from their Lenten class preparation for the Feast of Brightness, their young eyes missed nothing in that ring of wonder that hung like a silent blessing almost within reach of their small hands.

Their teacher joined them. I knew what she was thinking. Would she talk about God, about Easter, about a prayer of thanks? She didn't. Instinctively she knew that the still surprise of the children was already an act of worship – there was nothing more, just then, to add. To experience that tiny theophany was in itself to adore. And maybe that timeless moment had more to do with the transformation of our universe than we will ever know. 'It is only beauty', said Simone Weil, 'that will save the world. Beauty is a sacrament; it is Christ's tender smile coming through the world.'

The vocation of the priest is to be a prophet of beauty, to remind people of the light within them; to reassure them that they are, as Thomas Merton realised in his moment of intense disclosure in a city street, 'shining like the sun', to tell them, that they, like those schoolchildren, can almost touch a rainbow. The calling of the priest, like it was for Jesus before him, and like it is for the church and her sacraments now, is not to introduce something new to God's creation, but to reveal, purify and intensify what is already there.

I recently read *Years of Wonder* by Geraldine Brooks. It was the time of the seventeenth-century Great Plague in Eyam, Derbyshire. The small community heroically decided to close off all contact with the outside world so as to contain the deadly disease within their village. Most of them died horrible deaths. Towards the end of these fateful months, Mrs Mompellion, the vicar's wife, despite her illness, whispers these words of hope to her distraught, despairing helper, Anna: 'I wonder if you know how you have changed. It is the one good to have come out of this terrible year. Oh yes, Anna, the spark was clear in you when you first came to me – but you covered your light, afraid of what would happen if anyone saw it. You were like a flame blown by the wind until it is almost gone. All I had to do was to put the glass round you. And now, oh how you shine!'

At the splintered threshold-moments of their lives, the priest puts the glass around the fragile hearts of his people. And strange as it may seem, he may well have to walk across the broken glass of his own shattered vows before he can do this with a new innocence (*pace* R. S. Thomas). He knows that if he is ever to name, protect and reveal the mysterious place of beauty in others, he himself must first, like Anna, be broken and then put together again by loving hearts.

Irenaeus was talking about beauty when he said that the glory of God was the fully alive human being. So was St Paul when he reminds us that 'our unveiled faces reflect like mirrors the brightness of the Lord, growing brighter and brighter as we are turned into the image that we reflect'. And in the most wonderful words, Thomas Aquinas assures us that 'God is beauty itself, beautifying all things. God puts into creatures a kind of sheen, a reflection of God's own luminous ray, which is the fountain of all light.'

A few years ago, our parishioners organised 'A Day of Beauty' on the Sunday of the Transfiguration. We sent posters to other churches, put them in shop windows, placed news items in the local papers. It turned out to be a day of tears and smiles, of memories and dreams. Everything about that day was special, and all who came with their own creations of what was beautiful were pampered and spoiled and made to feel unique. Moira wrote to us afterwards: 'Bodies danced our yearning to reach God, and lovely stories led us into the invitation of the day – to recognise and trust the beauty in ourselves, awakened by the call of beauty from others. I felt my heart grow bigger, pushed outwards, full of thankfulness and wonder at this vision of what life can be like – much as I imagine James, John and Peter felt on the mountain that day.'

Few things in life have the compelling power of beauty. Beauty beckons us once we have recognised it. It points beyond itself. We know it is a sacrament of God because that is what the beautiful humanity of Jesus is. Beauty awakens us to our mystery and transforms us more deeply into it. It tells us our name and names our horizons. For beauty we are born. By beauty we are nourished. Without it we decay. Our seeds of beauty may sleep through many a winter, but they never die. Ronald Rolheiser reminds us that taking care of those seeds is priestly work.

At the deepest level of our being, we already know beauty and resonate sympathetically with it because we are ourselves beautiful. In the depth of our souls we carry an icon of the One who is Beautiful. We have within us the image and likeness of God, the source of all beauty. That *'Imago Dei'*, that deep virginal spot within us, that place where hands infinitely more gentle than our own once caressed us before we were born, where our souls were kissed before birth, where all that is most precious in us still dwells, where the fire of love still burns, and where ultimately we judge everything as to its love and truth – in that place we feel a *'vibration sympathetique'* in the face of beauty. It stirs the soul where it is most tender.

In Alice Walker's *The Color Purple*, Shug reminds us how fed up God must be when we walk through a field of poppies and fail to notice the colour purple. Rabbi Lionel Blue refers to an admonition in the Talmud. On the final Judgement Day we shall be called to account for all the beautiful things we should have enjoyed – and didn't. The Irish poet Patrick Kavanagh explains why a parish priest worried about the spirituality of his new curate. The younger man was never afraid when the sun opened a flower. Because sin is blind to beauty. It is grey, has no imagination and misses the purple.

Every priest is called to be a sacrament of the mystical, a reminder for people of their divine loveliness. There is a beautiful way of celebrating Eucharist, of preaching the Word, of being present to the hurting, of embracing sinners, of dancing with the limping on this precious Earth. The people will then believe that by their very presence, every word and every meal they share becomes a small but vibrant sacrament of God's beauty, warming people's hearts when they grow too cold, and bringing the morning early, when the nights are too dark and too slow. And that's when people will start going to Mass again.

If birthdays, anniversaries and sacred moments are celebrated in heaven, if ever the Lord of Life takes to the floor as Lord of the Dance, it must surely be at such poignant incarnations on this earth, of the everlasting beauty of our Tremendous Lover. Because, in the first instance, that is why the Word became flesh in Jesus.

Goodbye is a Small Death
The necessary losses that lead to abundance

In clerical circles, September is the month of 'moves'. It is that time of year when priests change their addresses. At the request of, or with the permission of, the bishop, they pack their things and push off to another parish.

This may be a tearful – or indeed a joyful! – occasion for both pastors and parishioners. This month, hundreds of priests and lay folk across the country will be going through a strange form of endings and beginnings, of death of the familiar and of preparing for the unknown.

It is important to honour the deep and hidden emotions that are experienced in the hearts of those who are affected by these happenings. Family-free, so much of the celibate priest's life can be packed into a few boxes of books and personal belongings, and transported to another just-evacuated house. But the working-out of emotions and the coming to terms with them cannot be completed in a couple of weeks. In the Catholic world, indelible and invisible traces are left in many lives when a priest leaves the parish that was his home and family.

There will always be something unique about the place of priests in the hearts of many parishioners. Priests are the ones who are privileged to serve people at those raw and sensitive experiences of utter darkness and of great joy. Whenever there is a mutual vulnerability at such timeless moments, unforgettable bonds are formed. We will always love those who hold us carefully, who touch us unerringly in the dark mystery of our loss, in the shy telling of our dreams. And we will always love those whose words, whose actions, whose very presence, give us permission to trust our hearts, to be intimate with a God who is hopelessly in love with us.

There is something within us that panics at the possibility of being left alone, or of striking out on our own. In all the crossing places of our lives I think that we die a little every time we empty a drawer that has become a reliable friend. At such irrevocable moments we can feel a faint tremble when we close the last suitcase. There are intimations of mortality when we turn the lock in anything familiar, for the last time; when we stop to look back, sometimes from the threshold, sometimes from a few yards or miles down the road, at the places and the people we are leaving. That is when, deep inside us, we hear again doors slamming along the corridors of our lives, every slam carrying echoes of past endings, past goodbyes to those who filled our lives, even for a little while, with a new love and a new possibility. Every parting secretly resonates with the womb that made us and the tomb that awaits us.

If we are made by God to love and be loved, to know and to be known, then is it any wonder that any threat to this essential destiny strikes very deep chords of terror? That is why, when it comes to any significant form of leaving, of letting go of relationships, of those unavoidable transitions where our hearts are concerned, there is an unprotected place in all of us. The heart's reactions and responses are not always logical. 'The heart has reasons that Reason knows not of.'

This deep existential fear we carry of loss and alienation starts early. In my last parish, a predecessor of mine, Fr Damian Webb OSB, pioneered invaluable research into the nursery rhymes and games of children. He revealed the presence of an intense anxiety about endings and death at a very early age in their psyches.

He gathered such knowledge from observing, among other activities, the hopping and skipping of small children over the cracks in the pavement, together with their chants about life and death, about escaping the devil waiting in the abyss for those who fell between the stone flags. Fr Damian's lifelong work serves only to underline the constant, innate apprehension that surrounds our moments of partings and endings.

At this stage I want to suggest the possibility of a strange transformation in our essential depth as human beings whenever we experience such transitions. Whether as departing parish priests, redundant employees, or anyone who for whatever reason has to cope with radical changes in their work and communities, there is often a rich source of growth and self-understanding in such unsolicited intrusions into our lives.

In most relationships, for example, especially family and friendship ones, there is seldom any way to avoid these necessary losses. It is the pattern of our existence in unpredictable time and space. There is a sense, however, in which only our absence can deepen and cleanse our presence. What I mean is that it may be better that we go away, on our own, for a week or for a year. Not all endings spell out only blank nothingness and empty loss. A persistent paradox is written into all the vicissitudes of our precarious lives and human bonding. There are many unlikely thresholds.

As parents, you experience this when your children grow up and move away. First there is the pain of letting them go. But eventually there is the joy of meeting those same children in a renewed way – as adults who can befriend you, and be with you, in a way that they could not as children.

The American lecturer and writer Fr Ronald Rolheiser writes: 'Good parents know that by hanging on too tightly, by not giving their children the space within which to be absent, they not only stunt their growth, but they deprive themselves of eventually having a wonderful adult come back to them, with something deeper to give than the dependent love of a child. And that is true of every relationship.'

The same author reflects that when children leave home for the first time to begin lives on their own, in one fashion or another, they are saying to their parents what Jesus said to his disciples before his Ascension: 'It is better for you that I go away. If I do not go away I cannot come back to you in a deeper way.' We speak those words, too, every time we walk out of a door, for years or days, and have to say the word 'goodbye'. What is important to remember at every such moment of letting go, is that a secret, eternal smile of memory lives on in our hearts.

One October evening, feeling unusually vulnerable to everything, I was returning fairly late to the presbytery. I noticed a falling leaf, swaying and dancing around me in the glow of the street light. In a moment I reached a new awareness of the mysterious descent of the leaf from the tree. There is a split second when, ever so gently, each leaf lets go, at its vital stem, of the only contact with its source of life on the branch. What an awful, ordinary moment! So, too, with all of us, I reflected, as intimations of our own mortality echo in our souls. 'I wish I knew the beauty of leaves falling,' the poet David Ignatow wrote, 'To whom are we beautiful as we go?'

But that evening I noticed, too, the new dancing of the finally liberated leaf. It seemed to be lightly playing a deadly serious game of immortality – like all dancers, who, quick on their feet, refuse to acknowledge the downward pull of the gravity of death, holding themselves in perfect balance between heaven and earth. A Celtic phrase of hope brought a small smile to my fragile face. I likened the hint of wildness in the concept of heaven, after that final letting go, the *Siamsa Dé*, the divine fiesta for the new arrivals, led by the Lady and Lord of the Dance themselves.

Echoes of Intimacy

We reveal and reflect their creativity to Mother Earth and Mother God

'I want,' she said, 'to live more deeply. My life is flat. It has no echoes.' It was the kind of remark you tend to remember. With several painful relationships behind her, and a dismal Scottish tour with a doomed country and western trio, Shirley was now searching for a more meaningful life.

As often happens, late at night after long days, certain words, faces and moments flash across my mind before I go to sleep. Shirley's poetic, spontaneous little soul-cry reminded me of many empty moments in my own life, moments when I feel trapped in my blindness, quarantined within my own limitations. Something reachable remains just beyond my grasp; something attainable beckons from too far away.

The last time it happened was when I was travelling west along the M62. Just where the sign says 'You are now at the highest motorway point (372m) in England', I pulled over and looked around me at the long vista of the Yorkshire Dales stretching for ever to distant horizons on both sides of me. With the changing light, the shifting shadows and the sudden mists, I sensed an enchanted world out there, but one from which I felt excluded.

It was then that I began again to fret because I could not really feel part of that spare beauty around me. I could not enter into it, resonate with it, be fulfilled by it, expand with it, flow with it. It was as though an invisible filter blurred its impact on my soul; as though I were a spectator at something out there, distant and detached. There was no resonance between us, no 'echoes', as Shirley had put it. My distress was nothing new. In recent years I have grieved over the loss of some magical qualities I had enjoyed as a child.

As I sat and reflected somewhat anxiously on these things, two lines of thought arose, in quick succession, in my mind. They emerged as a pair of disarmingly simple images calling me into another more contemplative way of looking at things. One – what I call the mirror image – sprang from a belief about the part that each one of us plays in the continuing story of our growing world. As I was gazing at the undulating hills of heather, I tried to see myself as a mirror reflecting back to Mother Nature what she looked like, through the eyes of her own child, me. 'Reflecting in the consciousness of each one of us', wrote Teilhard de Chardin, 'evolution is becoming aware of itself.' At some point creation became reflexive in giving birth to the human mind. This mind, according to John O'Donoghue, 'is the mirror in which creation can behold itself. In the human mind the earth becomes conscious and aware.'

Half-felt intimations were now becoming more clear. I saw myself as begotten by the world itself, flesh of her flesh and now needed by her, to bring home to her the unique beauty of her ever-changing face. Our human eyes feed back to Mother Earth what she looks like in every turning of the world's light. Without this moment the song of life would be forever unfinished, the universal story incomplete. These faint whisperings are too far-fetched for some: they are utterly and mystically natural for those others who feel in their bodies and souls the same heartpulse as the universe.

So there, in that high lay-by, I thought, 'I am a mirror for Gaia.' (Thus named by the Greeks who saw the earth as a living, sensitive, growing mother; a term brought to current usage by the scientist James Lovelock and celebrated now by many of our best theologians.) Without us she would never know her allurement, never delight in the beauty that captivated the souls of her human family. We have sprung from her womb. A spirituality of creation forever reminds us of this truth. Something dies when it is forgotten. That afternoon a lost intimacy was restored when I felt myself to be my earth mother's mirror; a weakened bond was strengthened when I rejoiced in this special gift I could lay before her. In the grand scale of things I had my unique and necessary role to echo uniquely back to her what she could not see for herself. 'Welcome home,' she says, 'I have missed and mourned you. Where have you been?'

As the eyes are to the body, so are we to the cosmos – and to God. This brings me to my second image – the window. God created the world so as eventually to become human in it, and therefore to enjoy all human experiences. God so loved the world that God assumed human nature in order to enjoy it. The incarnational theology of the mystics holds that if God is to continue rejoicing in that created divine beauty, then all our eyes and senses are needed to be windows of wonder for God on to the strange beauty of, for instance, even those lonely moors and peat bogs.

The Risen Christ told St Teresa that he needed her eyes to look with love on people and places. 'The real aim', wrote Simone Weil, 'is not to see God in all things; it is that God, through us, should see the things that we can see.' And touch the things that we can touch. And hear the things that we can hear. The theological giant Karl Barth, somewhat infatuated with the music of Mozart, surmised that when the horn concerto is on at full swell, 'then our dear Lord listens with special pleasure'. And do we dismiss too soon the stories of children playing their drums for God, or squeezing God in next to them for a ride and a chat in their new red and shiny fire-engines? After all, 'God is sheer joy,' wrote St Thomas Aquinas, when asked why God made the world, 'and sheer joy demands company.'

In *Sheep Fair Day*, Kerry Hardy writes:
I took God with me to the sheep fair. I said, 'Look
there's Liv, sitting on the wall waiting;
these are pens, these are sheep,
this is their shit we are walking in, this is their fear.'
Then I let God sip tea, boiling hot, from a cup,
and I lent God my fingers to feel how they burned
when I tripped on a stone and it slopped.
'This is hurt,' I said, 'there'll be more.'

Such an awareness makes the familiar delightfully unfamiliar again. The senses become thresholds to the Mystery, revealing an astonishing immediacy and intimacy with the universe and its Creator. You find yourself doing things you haven't done since you were a child – chatting to God as you walk or drive along, pointing out this and that, as you round each new bend in the road. You re-enter, in a completely new way, the childhood of play and wonder you once lived – but left too soon.

And what will Shirley make of all of this? Will she dismiss it as too cerebral, too remote, or will it help her find, in some corner of her lonely heart, that eternal echo of intimacy for which she longs?

Does Darkness Win?

Christ, no stranger to desperation, rushes to embrace those who commit suicide

It happened in a country place. A local teenager had committed suicide. I was summoned to the scene immediately. It was a timeless moment I shall never forget. In the unearthly light of a pale moon rising into the October sky, the field seemed empty. The 4ft 6ins body of Brian was lying in the grass, a 3ft 6ins rifle by his side. A cow was licking his face. I could hear the unbearable screams of anguish from the house beyond the gate.

Some years later I befriended Michael, a young postman, who had struggled with depression for a long time. We used to have great chats. I loved his company. On his rounds, one grey and silent morning, he parked his van, and walked heavily, through the long rushes, into a lonely lake.

Memories of those dreadful moments came back to me with alarming clarity when I visited a parishioner last week. His wife had committed suicide more than a year ago. He is still struggling to cope. He knows it will take a long time. It is for him, for the parents of Brian and Michael, and for the millions whose lives have been touched by suicide, that I offer these reflections as we approach November, that mysterious month of memories that both bless and disturb our souls.

On a 'good' day I cannot grasp how any kind of pressure could be intense enough to drive someone to seriously think about suicide. And on another personally dark day of quiet desperation, I can. You may remember the fairly recent collapse of the Enron empire. Not long afterwards a top executive killed himself. Why would this man end his life while many others, in even far more disgraceful or disastrous circumstances, would manage to hang on and survive? Probably because they would unmask and recognise their shame and self-blame; they would search, in spite of their desolation and fear, for a truer perspective on the whole issue; they would try to weigh up the longterm consequences, and painfully find a new way forward – a way that might eventually be more fulfilling than anything they had lost.

My own suggestion is that without being held, in love, in some sense or another, this slow climb back into the light is impossible. People's inner reaction to tragedy varies so much. In the soul of that Enron leader, perhaps the identity of success, power and human respect was stronger than the identity of his own humanity as husband, father, community member, son of God? All of this is very unsure ground on which to be speculating about the inner worlds of a person's soul – that fragile, fearful place – so strong on a Sunday, so anxious on a Monday.

There is something about the news of a suicide that cuts across everything we are doing or thinking. It has a chilling ring to it. We are stopped in our tracks. Everything else becomes unimportant. With deep gut reaction, we know that there is something ultimate here. There is no pretence in the minds of those who take their own lives. Somewhere in all of us, a silent shiver of fear begins. Most letters received by counselling services concern this phenomenon. Either intimately, or at a distance, almost all of us are personally acquainted with the shock of suicide.

You may remember the tragedy last year, when Dr David Kelly took his own life. He felt caught in a tangle that made it impossible for him to live any more. By all accounts he was strong and gentle, a good man, a true friend, a father and husband. And something snapped. The strain, the pain, the unbearable pressure were all too much. Before he died, the scientist referred to those 'dark players in a deadly game'.

Closer to home, any one of us is liable to be seduced into the power games of dark players in our own community, in our own family, in our own mind. And I'm always surprised at the number of my own acquaintances who are prepared to admit that, maybe even briefly and superficially, they have, at some stage in their lives, considered the possibility of ending it all.

There is so much mystery about the inner state of those hearts and minds that cannot go on with the journey of life. It is foolish to pass judgement too soon. Grace is everywhere. Earlier this year we read another suicide story about a man who was referred to as an agent of evil. In *The Independent* Paul Vallely wrote, 'Harold Shipman's suicide raises an intriguing question.

Was the fact that he took his own life evidence that even a man like him was capable of a transforming journey?'

With all its profound complexities, the propensity for suicide is, in most cases, an illness. We are made up of body and soul; either can snap. Fr Ronald Rolheiser, whose sensitive understanding of this phenomenon I incorporate in this article, wrote, 'We can die of cancer, high blood pressure, heart attacks, aneurysms. These are physical sicknesses. But we can suffer those, too, in the soul. There are malignancies and aneurysms also of the heart – mortal wounds from which the soul cannot recover.'

When a person commits suicide it is always a tragedy, but not always an act of despair. The death is not freely chosen, but is a desperate attempt to end unendurable pain. And there is no reason for the deep guilt and self-blame that sometimes haunts the lives of those who are left behind. We often torment ourselves by regretting not being there when the tragedy happened. But we were not there for the very reason that the person did not wish us to be there. He or she chose the time and place precisely with our absence in mind. That is part of the anatomy of the disease of suicide. And, this side of heaven, sometimes all the outstretched hands and professional help in the world cannot reach a heart paralysed by fear and illness.

Our wounded loved ones, who fall victim to suicide, are safe in God's huge heart – safer by far than at the hands of those of us who, in our ignorance, tend to judge and condemn. The Christian response to suicide should not be horror, or fear for the person's salvation. Suicide victims are met by a gentle Christ who, with a compassionate embrace, restores peace to their troubled hearts.

Neither should we be anxious, or forever accusing ourselves, about what we did, or did not do, or whether, if we had paid enough careful attention, we could have prevented the tragedy. Such understandable but self-defeating introspection brings no healing. What friends can do is gently hold the grieving ones, share their helplessness, avoid explaining, carefully harvest the bits and pieces of today's hope to make tomorrow's living a possibility. They can encourage the person to talk, be prepared to listen and place some reasons for living into an empty-looking future.

Suicide is, indeed, a desperate way to die, but we must understand it for what it is, a sickness of the soul. And the God who redeems all manner of failures and mistakes, who brings new light into even the deepest darkness, will restore eternal hope and courage to those frightened hearts who leave this life too early.

Tyranny of Perfection
To be excessively anxious is to miss the whole point of Salvation

I was 'doing supply' for my brother who was chaplain to a psychiatric ward in a large hospital in Manchester. One night the bleeper summoned me to the bedside of Maria. When I arrived the doctor explained, 'This patient is deeply disturbed by what she calls her sins and imperfections. She feels she is not in the state of grace, whatever that may mean. Her acute anxiety stems from an obsession with being perfect, from a fear of being punished. Maybe only a priest can heal her religious guilt.'

I realised that the patient was suffering from a 'Catholic neurosis', a distressing state brought on by bouts of scrupulosity. It used to drive sensitive souls to distraction. After sixty years I still remember in detail going back twice to the same priest, in the same confession box, in the same afternoon, because, after many efforts, I failed to say my penance perfectly, that is, without distractions. 'Too late now,' he testily replied, 'it's only the first attempt that counts.' I have little doubt that the terror I felt at those words still reverberates somewhere within me.

I spoke a lot with Maria. A particular brand of piety had fuelled tormenting thoughts about her personal sinfulness, her fear of God's anger, and finally had unbalanced her mind. She felt she had to earn God's forgiveness by being perfect. To be her normal, human self was to incur divine anger and risk going to hell. There are those who now refer to these experiences as examples of spiritual abuse.

Children are defenceless in the face of such dangerous beliefs. They are notoriously quick to blame themselves. They are rendered powerless from the beginning, when their inner, natural confidence and self-esteem are relentlessly eroded by inaccurate and inappropriate teaching about original sin and our complicity in the crucifying of Jesus. Not many older Catholics can remember being told, when they were small, that God's explosive and unconditional love was flowing into, and out of, their lives like an eternal river. Or that God was madly in love with them.

The innocent young heart of Maria could not take any more of that destructive caricature of a punishing God. So it went into hibernation for a long, long winter. It was, I remember, a hard journey that both of us then had to face, first unlearning all the negative untruths that had obscured the sun of God's unconditional love from her fearful heart. And then, as sure as dawn follows night, came the blessed release. All that was needed was the unblocking. The light of God, still flickering in her sensitive heart, slowly but inevitably grew stronger by the day.

Her fears, of course, kept returning. The tapes from early parenting, religious education and Sunday preaching would still play relentlessly in her head. But a stronger music was now gathering its own irresistible rhythm. It was the rhythm and beat of her own natural humanity, already fashioned in the invincible image of God. It was the rhythm and beat of the indelible graces of the Trinity at the core of her being – graces that were first celebrated at her baptism when she was delightedly anointed priestess, prophetess and princess within the intimacy of God's family.

But only now, and almost too late, were these true and breathtaking affirmations emerging. What this woman's aching heart was waiting to be told all through her winter of waiting was how loved she was; how precious she was to God; how utterly inconsequential were her so-called sins before the love of God.

But was I sure, she would keep asking me, because those tapes were carrying a different message. And repeatedly I would reply: 'Just look at Jesus – look nowhere else. Look at his beautiful human heart. Reflect on the extravagance of his love and forgiveness. There, and there only, will you find the true heart of God.'

Over the past few years I have often reflected on this encounter. Every week I meet those who still carry guilt, shame or anxiety about the state of their lives. They feel they should be better than they are. They struggle with those wayward parts of themselves that they cannot 'control'. They blame themselves for not being perfect.

Sometimes I discuss with those troubled souls (and that means most of us) the possibility that we are trying too hard to be good. I suggest to them that, no matter what, there will always be a certain, difficult load to carry. 'To be human is to be flawed, to be in conflict, to be unfinished.' Here, and here alone, does the grace of trust find its place – trust in life, trust in love, trust in a God who doesn't have a problem with our imperfection. What I mean is that there is little point in trying to be perfect. Ordinary human beings just don't do perfection very well. Nor are we meant to – for the simple reason that this is how God has made us. 'Perfection', wrote Simone Weil, 'is sterile; it cannot have children.'

We would never know light if we never experienced darkness. We could never know love if we never experienced fear. Nor would we ever forgive if we had never been hurt. The challenge is not to get rid of the shadows and flaws; the challenge is to somehow recognise the hurts, accept them, befriend them, and then integrate them into the rest of our lives. That is what Jesus was doing throughout his time with us. He was always trying to make himself holy, to hold the weeds and wheat of life together. In the journey of his fragile soul, he swung and swayed, in intense torment, between giving in to, and resisting, his temptations; between refusing and accepting the chalice of his destiny.

Jesus was shockingly human. On our inner journey, we too are called only to be ourselves, to be grateful for the bagful of eccentric and often scary bits and pieces that make up our complex and complicated personalities. Not all sins are that bad! There is an explosive revelation hidden within the Easter Exultet, when we greet the sin of Adam as a 'happy, necessary fault'.

When we struggle too hard to be perfect, we only lose heart quickly. When we attack the faults and foibles that inhabit our souls, we only make them more subtle, more potentially damaging. Strangely enough, the best advice may be to welcome them all! I like to believe that even the most fearful and threatening things that prowl around the perimeters of our inside spaces are all bringing us some kind of gift. Maybe that is what Jesus meant when he said 'Love your enemies'.

It is not a very wise thing to do, then, to strive to cut out of ourselves those parts that cause us trouble. We don't cut out, or cut off, those parts of our bodies that are unhealthy; we work towards their healing. There is no point in denying what is truly essential to us, in ripping out all that isn't 'good'.

It is that way, too, with the things of the spirit. What is banished only grows again, returns again, like those seven demons in the gospel, more threatening and aggressive than before. Maybe, then, we should think again about being too neat and clean and all swept up! Long live a little wilderness for the wildlife within us to grow. Nobody told Maria that.

Is Anybody There?

Do we feel the presence of our departed loved ones – waiting for us?

'If you've shares in limbo, sell immediately.' This piece of theological advice was already circulating around the catechetical markets of the seventies. At the time of going to press, Rome has still to speak definitively. Things don't move as fast in theological circles as in financial ones. What, then, about shares in purgatory? Like the limbo saga, this will be a long story.

Mystery surrounds what happens after death. During a parish mission this September a teacher tearfully told us her story. She and her friends had grieved the death of their colleague, by her own hand, last Christmas Day. Just recently, however, each of them was experiencing a new and great distress, sensing the troubled presence of their friend around them, as though waiting for something vital.

Parish priests suggest that such phenomena are happening more frequently now. The current TV series *Afterlife* stirs up our deepseated preoccupation with this whole mystery of connections between the spirits of the dead and our own. The plea of a thirty-six-year-old woman was featured in the run-up to the supernatural drama starring Lesley Sharp. '[I'm] smothered in sleep by a violent husband, now also dead. I'm trapped with him and he won't let me go. Someone help please.'

For many Catholics the plight of confused and needy departed souls was brought to our attention at a very early age. High on holy adrenalin, we would meet every hour or so in the church porch, to compare notes. Or rather numbers. Let me explain. My memories, just now, are back in the Novembers of the fifties. Every time, on All Souls' Day, that we made separate visits to a designated church and recited certain prayers, a soul would fly free from purgatory. (Catholics of a certain age will remember the prescribed conditions for procuring such an 'indulgence'.) After each urgent visit we would dash out of the church again, sprint briefly down the path (thus ensuring that the next visit was a separate one) and then crash back through the still-swinging doors to rescue another tormented prisoner. That evening, by the time the autumn shadows slanted sideways among the nearby graves, we would, all tired out, like latter-day Robin Hoods, gaze modestly at the darkening skies, now lit up by delighted spirits, shouting and dancing their way home.

Long before the emergence of Roman Catholicism in these islands, there was a pre-Christian Celtic sensitivity to the intermingling of the living and the dead, those who belonged to the present human race and those who were members of the *slua sídhe*, the people of the underworld. Their comings and goings were frequent, especially at the perennial 'turning-time' of *Samhain*. For them, heaven and earth, life and death, were not mutually exclusive, chronologically different or categorically distinct modes of being. In the mythology of the *Tuatha Dé Dannan*, for instance, it is believed that those who die do not so much disappear away from this world as become a more essential dimension of it. Death integrates rather than ends.

'There is an ambiguity here,' writes Dr Noel Dermot O'Donoghue, 'that Christian theology from the time of Augustine until today, has never quite resolved. Are the dead alive in another region, or do they somehow, somewhere, await an awakening? Are they still somehow part of nature, or do they dwell in a spirit-world which may be near to us but is yet of a totally different substance? Are the men and women who walked the hills of Dana, and laboured in its fields and uplands, now without any presence in this place, now unremembering and unconcerned?'

At the foot of these very hills, an elderly brother and sister asked me to visit them one foggy October evening. They wanted to tell me about the ghost who regularly came to sit near their open fire without uttering a word. Anxiously they were wondering if it might be one of their ancestors in search of, or in need of, some release, or justice, or prayers. Was there something unfinished in his earthly life that had to be completed? Was he one of those still lost in the swirling mists of his winter crossing? And why might this be?

As a recluse will stumble back into the shadows of dark familiarity, blinded by the honesty of the noonday sun, does the premature soul recoil in some kind of shock – until it is ready for the shining? Could this be the reason that Catholics, in the face of a certain Protestant opposition, insist that 'it is a holy and a wholesome thought to pray for the dead'? The sinister surroundings of those who have died, and our ability to bring them light and comfort, may be stronger than we think. The vital life forces at the heart of creation continue to flow beyond death. Maybe without our purest, most selfless prayers they cannot face the flat desert of cutting winds between here and there, and so they flee back to sit by someone's fireside in the hills of Dana for another season of waiting. Maybe purgatory is just a name for the dark materials at large when the soul wrestles with its last temptation.

Buddhists celebrate *satanga* – a universal gathering of past and present souls. Buddha was once giving a talk in the forest and he asked his disciples to make room for the many invisible visitors that had come to listen. 'You cannot see them', he said, 'but the forest is filled with spirits at this moment.'

Especially in November evenings, there is a way of sensing in the movements of the elements the living presence of the dead around us. Maybe the beyond is in the midst. Maybe people die into the world rather than out of it. A shiver still slides down my spine when I recall Walter de la Mare's *The Listeners*. He describes the silent host of spirits that 'stood thronging the faint moonbeams on the dark stair' of the eerie inn, and the grim Traveller at the door who came back 'to keep his word'.

In his poem *All Hallows*, David Scott writes about the priest preparing the altar for a Nuptial Mass. A few people had arrived and everything seemed normal …

… Until counting out the bread, I looked
and saw the church was full of people, all alert and tall and
ready.
Some long dead have now returned to sing,
some recent friends, all light and shining
in the latticed sun. I could not move
for those that loved the place.
They needed welcoming, and so I stepped
beyond the rubrics, and said my stumbling piece:

'how they had as much a right as we,
how valued for their clothes of white and gold
and pale green'. Only half was I remembering
the wedding and the followers that
just the day before had been arranged
with never this in mind.

Seeds of Desire

Made in God's astonishing image, we can never settle for less

Some things you don't easily forget. I still remember a special moment from around this time last year. Their small faces ablaze with innocence, Kaitlin and Matilda lit the first purple candle in our Advent wreath. Something about the way they shyly smiled at each other was already providing us with a glimpse into the mystery for which we were preparing. What I was feeling was a kind of aching and longing. The focus shifted from the external rubric to the inner reality. A silent chord was struck. 'Who looks outside dreams,' wrote Carl Jung, 'who looks inside awakens.'

When I was a child we needed a freshwater well at home. I can still remember the water diviner, in total concentration, as he walked across our small yard. Like horsewhisperers and alchemists, he had 'the gift'. At one with his lightly held twig, he 'divined' the presence of the sweetest water deep down in the earth, waiting to rush free and fast to the surface for our family and neighbours.

On that wintry Sunday, Kaitlin and Matilda, too, had 'the gift'. In one innocent instant, they had enabled us to 'divine' our divinity, to sense God's indelible image within even the most careless and sinful of us that morning. Theirs was a ministry of discovery – that deep down, below the rubble and sins of our lives, runs that underground river of God's faithful devotion: that, hidden beneath the unyielding land of our daily existence, run the veins of gold.

This is the holy work of the church – to find the hidden well of mystery within us; to recover, when we are lost, the revelation of our own shrouded beginnings. We forget our destiny. God's dream for us remains unremembered. I like to think of the priest in Advent as the guide up ahead, the spy deep inside, who charts and discerns with us the terrain, the horizons and the substance of our lives through the filter of Incarnation. 'The priest is a poet and more,' Karl Rahner wrote, 'the poet listens to life. The priest listens to life under the influence of the Word.'

One reason why Advent carries such a tangible impact is its

potential response to the existential longing that never stops nagging at our human souls. A lust to live life to the full, to love like the greatest lovers, courses relentlessly in our bloodstreams. Everything about us is constantly tinged with an incessant yearning for some indefinable reality. This raw and relentless compulsion to transcend our own mortality is the restlessness of the indwelling Holy Spirit, drawing us towards the heart of God. Robert Browning wrote 'Ah! But a man's reach must exceed his grasp, or what's a heaven for?'

The liturgy of the Christian Church, at its best, responds to this mystery of our inner truth. In preparation for Advent, for instance, the opening prayers of the final Sundays in Ordinary Time carry phrases such as 'Lead us to seek beyond our reach', 'Our longing for your presence is more than for life itself ', 'The love you give us always exceeds the furthest expression of our human desire'.

Sometimes, however, our rubrical niceties take on a false life of their own, trivialising and obscuring their very real and necessary function. Too many pretty para-liturgies have lost all relevance to life. Advent is not about waiting for the baby Jesus as though nobody had told us he had already arrived. It is, rather, about trying to make sense of that intense and disturbing imperative for a completeness that always eludes us, that burns in our flesh and that never leaves us alone.

After all, as Meister Eckhart insisted, we are all born with God's seed in us. Our lives are the womb that brings that seed to birth. The Advent moment – our lives in miniature – reminds us that we are coded for God; we are programmed for heaven; we are an incompleteness searching for completeness. As rivers flow and winds blow, so, too, the human heart, with its imagination, affections and creativity, will never be – cannot ever be – other than God-bound. *Corda nostra – capax mundi, capax Dei.* Advent paints for us a picture of the ultimate horizon of our longings. It holds up before us the mirror-image of our destiny. (Maybe that is what moved us when Kaitlin and Matilda brought a ray of bright colour into our November lives.)

But, in the very same breath, the first readings of Advent also waken us up to the danger of arriving home too soon, of settling, prematurely, for lesser unions, or, in scriptural imagery, of 'missing the mark', mistaking false gods for God. Because the universal, relentless allurement towards intimacy within all of us is so strong, we are easily seduced out of true. The sin, then, lies not in the pursuit of the fulfilment of our days and nights but in the setting up of the shop of our lives at the wrong address, in misreading 'true north' in the compass of our brief existence on this earth.

Advent reminds us of, and returns us to, our true roots, to God's first dream for us. It traces our family tree in the genealogy of Matthew. The infancy of Jesus is the infancy of all of us. That is why our hearts are restless until they rest in God. But the bother is that we forget. A strange shadow called original sin obscures the original vision of our holy heritage. A routine darkness falls across the window of our bright destiny.

There is a story that might help us here, about a church in the Netherlands. On entering the building, everyone would stop and bow in the direction of a whitewashed wall. It was a tradition that nobody questioned. They felt it was the right thing to do. One day the parish decided to renovate the church. They began to strip the paint off the old walls. While doing this they discovered traces of a painting on the wall towards which everyone bowed, but nobody knew why. Very carefully they peeled off the layers of whitewash. What emerged was an ancient, and very beautiful, painting of Christ. Nobody was old enough to have actually seen it. But now they came to understand why they almost instinctively persisted in honouring the wall that concealed the glorious work of art. The holy work of Advent is, I think, a little like that. It peels away the false veneer to reveal and restore under our December anxiety and excitement the unique masterpiece that underpins, inspires and echoes the eternal longing of every human/divine heart.

And the shock of seeing that original masterpiece should turn our lives upside down. 'Make ready for the Christ', wrote Thomas Merton, 'whose smile, like lightning, sets free the song of everlasting glory that now sleeps, in your paper flesh, like dynamite.' But it is all so overwhelming. It is too disturbing and frightening. Like Mary, we struggle with the challenge of the invitation. Can this really be true? Is this the destiny for which our hearts have been searching?

In the Opening Prayer of the first Sunday in Advent, we ask that 'our longing may be increased'. Maybe God will take us at our word and send along another Kaitlin and Matilda to light a candle. And maybe its light will reach our waiting womb. And then, with Mary and her cousin Elizabeth, when we trust those stirrings within us, a new creation begins, and our awakening life, like theirs, will leap within us for joy.

Horizons of the Heart
We are called into the deep by God's dream for us

Barrie and Tish, two of our parishioners in their early fifties, bought a boat this summer and are now sailing for Turkey. It was something they wanted to do for a long time. It will take them a couple of years to complete the adventure. Their regular 'Postcards from the Sea' are shared in our weekly newsletter. Last week they reported the repair, at Marseilles port, of a smashed mast, and now Combava is sailing, once more, on her way across the Mediterranean Sea.

There are many ways of launching into the deep. There are moments in our lives when the yearning for radical change becomes especially intense. This insistent whisper may not be immediately recognised by everyone. But, given the divine source of our true essence, I suspect that it is always there. Something within us, maybe at the most unlikely times, and at our deepest and most hidden levels, keeps convincing us, and often with a relentless urgency, of distant but reachable horizons.

Is this what John Paul II was referring to when, before he died, he urged us to take risks? *Duc in altum.* Is it true to say that without this desire, whether faint or focused, we are stuck in a stagnant religion, dammed-up in a fairly infantile faith? So many believers are corralled into a programmed and seemingly safe way of being Christian. Yet, almost paradoxically, it is only in a deeply rooted faith that we find the source and summit of this silent yearning for a richer, and more risky way of following the call of our hearts. Our churches have still within them faithful people who are burning with an unconscious longing to fly into other skies.

I'm a Capricorn. On my wall is a picture of a determined-looking goat midway through a huge leap across a terrifying chasm. As I complete my current move to another presbytery, I pause before it every day. Because that's where I find myself during these months of my life – looking for a place to land. At this point of the launching out into the unknown, to another way of ministering as a priest, the secret is in not looking down-wards or backwards, in not losing heart. In the transitions of our lives, there is a fatal attraction to the void below. There is such a safety about the familiar routines that they provide us with a false identity. It is unavoidable, then, in our pursuit of authentic-ity, that our ego should spread anxious panic. But the felt fear only testifies to the risk we are taking and the courage we are embracing. We will always be tempted to doubt, to look down, to look back. There have been times in all the crossing-places of my own life when I battled with the cautioning tapes of parents, teachers and priests still turning in my head. It was then that I wanted to return to the safety of the status quo, to retrace my steps back down along the slow paths of my recent ascent, where the embers of the previous evenings' camp-fires were still warm.

When I listen to the hidden dreams of ordinary, healthy peo-ple I often wonder whether this persistent compulsion for greater and finer things burns in every human heart. (A recent review reveals that millions of Britons – over a quarter of all 30-50 year olds – are currently considering such an option, even though in most cases it involves a decrease in income.) All kinds of counter-attractions – loss of nerve, negative judgements and jealous comments – can numb out and dumb down that first God-given spark that is always waiting to be fanned into a fiercer flame. But that spark, I believe, can never be extin-guished. God's imagination is incarnate within us. It is not easily overcome. 'Creative minds have always been known to survive any kind of bad training,' wrote Anna Freud. The anthropolo-gist Mary Daly reminds us that the creative potential itself in human beings is the enfleshed restlessness of the deity. It is im-portant to believe that we all carry within our bodies and hearts God's own dissatisfaction with the closed, lukewarm and safe ways of living. The whole thrust of every moment of Jesus' life was towards a passion for the possible.

I have come to believe that when we struggle to discern the pros and cons of making a leap into the unknown, there is a sense in which some part of us has made the move already. Something, in fact, has already happened upfront at the bound-aries of our life where the burning is brightest. A part of us has already crossed over into that as yet unknown space. It is waiting for the other parts of us to catch up. 'You must give birth to your images,' wrote the German poet Rainer Maria Rilke, 'They are the future waiting to be born. Fear not the strangeness you feel. The future must enter into you long before it happens.'

We have always carried the vague shape of a potential destiny somewhere within us – in our memory, in the unconscious, touched on in some of our more profound experiences. In an ultimate sense, I suppose that this is nowhere more true than in the intimations of our immortality that may strike us during these November days. We suddenly and fleetingly sense that a distant homecoming has already happened.

Is there, I wonder, something of immense importance hidden in the least of the aspirations of our lives? Antonio Machado, the Spanish poet, wrote, 'Anyone who moves onwards, even a little, walks, like Jesus, on the water.' Yet my own experience of walking on water resembles more the embarrassing misfortune of Peter than the quiet elegance of Jesus. To step out of the boat of our secure lives on to a precarious surface that may not hold our weight is a very foolhardy thing to do. Crossing a new terrain, to do a new work, is never a safe option. But once you begin to know yourself, to feel the shape of your soul, to have one courageous conversation with your true essence, then you have no choice. We are divinely created for growth; fashioned from the very beginning to become like God. That is why, to have heard the whisper of that call coming to you, like a far wave, is already to have answered.

When I take the risks of change, when I jump out of the boat like Peter, in spite of the grim, relentless tapes of caution that spool around in my memory, something deeper is there too. It is an intimation that I am always safely held. Our God-created nature guards us well. I take and hold the one hand that I know belongs in mine. So did Peter. And so did Jesus. Everything sustains your courage when your reach exceeds your grasp; when you step where you have never stepped before.

This is when, in the words of the Yorkshire poet David Whyte, we place our identity at the edge of discovery. It is time to move from an old life, before some kind of numbness sets in, making transition impossible. We die too soon when our work has no grace in it, no surprise, no inspiration; when it only maintains and bolsters up a soulless system. When our work is creative, the invisible becomes visible. But of this be sure: it will not be easy and others will not understand. You must follow your own star. I wonder if the seas are kind and the stars are bright for Tish and Barrie tonight.

Space for Grace

'Out beyond right and wrong, there's a field. I'll meet you there'

Being claustrophobic, November is not my favourite month. It is when my nightmares are most vivid, as I panic in small, dark tunnels, filled with an unbearable terror. And always, when travelling, anxiety grips me whenever I cannot get the aisle seat, the seat near the emergency exit, the seat nearest the door. I love spaces, vast expanses, unending horizons, seascapes and big windows.

There is a huge, flat field within a mile of the presbytery where I now live. It stretches for miles in all directions. I spoke to the farmer. He said it was designated on the flight-path map of pilots as a good place for an emergency landing. For the doomed descending, the field of space becomes the field of grace. I mention this huge, open field only because I love to stand in the middle of it – a place without limitations. I cannot wait to see the pure evenness of it when the sky covers it with snow. Because space is not a vacuum. More like an invitation to the imagination, a formless womb for holding mystery.

I remember a conversation I had with Vincente, the architect who built our most beautiful Church of St Benedict in East Leeds a few years ago. Behind the altar and the presidential chair we created a huge, totally empty wall. Parishioners thought we had forgotten something. Everyone wanted to pin a meaning on it – a figure, a banner, a text, a cross. Vincente talked to us about the potential for worship in the concept of space; about creating a building in which all that was unnecessary was excluded; about simplifying a church so that the emptiness could be made meaningful only by the infinite. The invisible as the strongest presence of all.

Karl Rahner wrote: 'There is no such thing, either in the world or in the heart, as literal vacancy, as a vacuum. And wherever space is really left by death, by renunciation, by parting, by apparent emptiness, provided the emptiness that cannot remain empty is not filled by the world, or activity, or chatter, or the deadly grief of the world – there is God.'

Thomas More, author of *Care of the Soul*, has written about the concept of *temenos*. He describes it as the holding of a certain area as a special or sacred precinct. It is where room, not necessarily geographical, is kept for the holy, the enchanted. For the Greeks of the past, *temenos* was the spiritual area for what lies beyond the functional and the immediate. This sacred space was not to be filled, used or polluted in any way. Its sole reason was to protect a meeting of spirits, to be a threshold into another world of a more profound reality. The work of liturgy in particular, he writes, needs its unique *temenos* so as to be effective and transformative.

In our new St Benedict's Church we also left lots of room around the altar – for dancing. Space loves to be danced in. In his book *The Empty Space* the renowned theatre director Peter Brook writes about that creative space which is the prerequisite for action. Every performance, whether music, dance or drama, is a kind of prayer, born out of silence and space. Reflecting on the Irish passion for setdancing with its exhilarating little jumps and turns, its circling and bowing beneath another couple's arms into new free space, to face the next row of dancers, Micheál Ó Siadhail, in *A Fragile City*, remembers 'a scent of dizziness' followed by the regularly repeated realignment of the dancers across the waiting space:

And we unfold into our design.
I want to dance forever. A veil
Shakes between now-ness and infinity.
Touch of hands. Communal and frail.
Our courtesies weave a fragile city.

Every writer too must face the blank page. Paradoxically, the more economical he or she is in the filling of that page, the more powerful the writing and the greater his or her ability to speak to the human heart. John McGahern, one of Ireland's finest writers of spare, beautiful prose, said that the best writing is about suggestion, not statement. I sent a poem of mine to Michael McCarthy, a priest-poet friend, for comment. 'It suffers', he replied, 'from its desire to express itself totally. The first thing about poetry is that everything does not have to be said. Its discipline has to do with understatement and evocation.' In *Henry James*, R. S. Thomas, the Celtic poet of God's darkness, writes about 'the eloquence of the unsaid thing, the nobility of the deed not performed, the significance of an absence'.

When it comes to understanding the essence of the Gracious Mystery, silent space and empty nothingness have long been at the heart of the church's apophatic tradition – a non-negotiable reminder that all our descriptions of God will forever be well wide of the mark. The Being called Love can never be confined in small images, in small liturgies, in small churches. We are always tempted to lock God away in windowless places with low ceilings and high security; to pinpoint the divine presence with fallible compasses and dogmatic navigation systems. The Spirit of God will always need space to blow and dance where she will.

There are two such inner spaces for grace that I am learning to treasure. One has to do with the tiny but eternal space we make room for, when we hold off, even for a split second, the negative – even violent – reaction to a sudden hurt, allowing into our souls a sliver of saving light. In that tiny oasis we recover our almost-lost balance and centre, our precarious peace. It lasts the space of a breath – but hides a heaven. The other subtle space is equally soul-saving. It is the space we move to, to stop the deadly habit of judging everyone and everything – a common and destructive habit. This place of grace, rarely visited because it remains uncharted in the doctrinal maps of our salvation, is where we, too, hold before us Christ's compassionate understanding of the complexity of our lives. 'Out beyond right and wrong there's a field,' wrote Rumi. 'I'll meet you there.'

Only when we sink into the thought-less, sense-less, image-less space of contemplation, when we surrender, in great and graced trust, to the emptiness and nothingness of the void we call God, will we ever even begin to get a glimpse of God at work in both of these Advent moments. There is an unforgettable humility and respect in R. S. Thomas' *Via Negativa*:

Why no! I never thought other than
That God is that great absence
In our lives, the empty silence
Within, the place where we go
Seeking, not in the hope to
Arrive or find. He keeps the interstices
In our knowledge, the darkness between stars.

The Face of a Baby

If you dare to love, be prepared to grieve

It is 11.45 pm on Christmas Eve. Everything is ready – except the homily! Our church had fallen down, literally. We were trying to keep our parish family together in the school hall. The day was spent in taking care of the essentials – finding an ordinary table for a makeshift altar, replacing infant chairs with ones big enough for well-padded adults, coaxing the caretaker for adequate heating, extra lighting for the partially sighted, making space, amid the clutter, for readers and eucharistic ministers to manoeuvre, finding a piano and a microphone that worked.

As we started Mass, I was blaming myself for not having a homily prepared. When the assembled parishioners came to their feet for the gospel, I noticed a tiny baby, no more than a few days old, asleep in her mother's arms. An idea hit me. I spoke briefly about the Almighty Creator and Judge that we worshipped and feared. 'How frightening would it be', I asked, 'if this omniscient God thundered into our world just now?' I stooped down to lift aloft the small child, no bigger than my fist. 'There,' I said, 'there is the power of God. Who can be afraid of a God like that?'

There are many faces to a baby. When you think about it, a baby is an amazing symbol of both power and powerlessness. Or, perhaps, more accurately, of power within powerlessness. As I felt the totally trusting baby stir sleepily in my hands I thought about her utter vulnerability, her total trust. How ambiguous and paradoxical it all was. And how shocking, too. This is what love does. It gives away its power. It renders itself destructible. All of this runs against the grain of our competitive and controlling nature. How can weakness ever be understood as the secret of true love? With every birth we ask ourselves the same question.

When loving couples have a baby, their lives become as precarious as that of the baby of their love. The beauty they have created shatters their former security. Their lives are irrevocably transformed.

But that is what love is like. It surrenders. It has no more masks, no more expectations, no more certainties. The Bethlehem baby's defenceless presence, his shocking and precarious weakness, his over-turning of all our ideas about the nature of God, stun us into silence. It is in this sacred silence, during these few precious days, that the hard thoughts within us can soften, that the unforgiving walls of judgement and blame can crumble, that the cold shadows of our pride can be melted by the warmth of an infant's smile. Such is the power of a baby. As R. S. Thomas puts it:

When we are weak, we are
Strong. When our eyes close
On the world, then somewhere
Within us the bush
Burns. When we are poor
And aware of the inadequacy
Of our table, it is to that,
Uninvited, the guest comes.

There are so many reasons why our splintered world, with its broken dreams, sorely needs the life-giving good news revealed in the faces of a baby. Fearful and anxious, how urgently we await this revelation of God's accessibility in the fragile body of a child. Aggressive and violent, how much our trigger-happy leaders can learn from God's way of establishing peace in the open trust of a baby. At a time when anxious millions are only too familiar with the 'half-life' of mere existence, how life-giving it is to see, in a kicking, delighted infant, the call – and permission – for us too to 'go barefoot' into each day, to live our lives to the full abundance of Life incarnate. And, in a divided, greedy, world divided between rich North and poor South, how desperately we all need the ultimate example of simply possessing nothing so that others may simply live.

There is a cross, too, in the face of a baby, for love and pain are conjoined twins. 'And thy own soul a sword shall pierce.' I think of my mum's heart when she realised from my brother Joseph's face that he was a Down's syndrome baby. She must have glimpsed a life of pain to come for all the family. If you dare to love, be prepared to grieve. How right she was! The perennial infancy narratives do not hide the shadow of Good Friday that falls across the heart of the Christmas baby. In fact the story of the baby's birth is based on the death and resurrection of the grown man.

It follows that God's glory and beauty are revealed in poor, humble, hurting and self-effacing lives of faith and compassion. It can be fully present in failure, disgrace and ignominy. The mystery of God is disguised and veiled in the most hopeless places and people, in the margins of life, in the helplessness of a baby.

Babies transform us by not threatening us. They bless us with the inner freedom to be ourselves – just as they always are. A baby is an invitation that draws out what is best within us. We do not resist a baby's love; in fact, we sense we need it. Small wonder that God's redemptive self-emptying resulted in the wonder of a baby. And that Jesus, too, held up the child as the epitome of his mission and power. Babies heal us. 'The moment I first looked at my baby,' a young father told me, 'the stammer left me.' They transform what is negative so that it cannot be transmitted any more.

In saying 'Yes' to life, the child takes the 'now' and makes it special. Because it yearns for life, it is as if it is insatiably addicted to growing. The small child reaches for the moon through the windows of its wonder and it stirs us to do the same. The child does not quit on life. It has an indelible curiosity about tomorrow, a passion for the possible. It does not need to hope or believe. Like God incarnate, it delights, writes Thomas Aquinas, in the joy of simply being there.

Christmas is the celebration of the truth that God is always accessible within whatever is happening to us, not outside it; that if God cannot hold us in our sin and shame, then God is dead; that if God is not touching us in our weakness, then Christmas is a cruel joke. Cardinal Avery Dulles wrote: 'The Incarnation does not provide us with a ladder by which to escape the ambiguities of life and scale the heights of heaven. Rather it enables us to burrow deep into the heart of planet Earth and find it shimmering with divinity.'

A trusting God risked placing a powerless baby in human hands to reveal and 'earth' the essence of divine, vulnerable and unconditional love. Astonishing though this mystery is, we still need sacramental moments to keep reminding us of it. Otherwise, because we are congenitally forgetful of our destiny, the miracle would grow dim and distant.

These moments of revelation come to all of us in different ways. For a few of us it came during that Midnight Mass in a small Yorkshire school, when a trusting mother risked letting her baby into the clumsy hands of her parish priest. Such are the ordinary ways that the extraordinarily beautiful mystery will be remembered, and the perennial star will be re-lit – to warm and guide us through another year.

This is what Love does
God's passionate longing for human intimacy

It was a child's comment to her father that started me off on a whole new way of thinking about Christmas. I was studying in the United States at the time, and paying my way by 'doing supply' at a local parish in San Francisco. They were standing together in front of the crib. Her father heard her musing to herself, 'I wonder if God enjoys being a baby.' Especially around this time of Advent, the child's reflection often returns to me and fills my mind. These are the moments when I find the realisation of what Incarnation means simply overwhelming. The veil of the routine seasonal repetitions is briefly parted and the heart is caught off guard.

Another such moment happened last month. A Sunday paper offered a free pre-Christmas DVD of an old film. In 1987 Wim Wenders won Best Director at Cannes for *Wings of Desire*. Wenders' post-war Berlin is full of ponytailed angels who listen to, and comfort, the broken hearts and minds of mortals. On the verge of falling in love with a beautiful trapeze artist, one of them, Damiel, becomes fascinated (against holy orders) with the possibility of becoming human. Told from the angels' point of view, the film is shot in black and white, blossoming into colour only when the angels perceive the realities of humankind.

It is wonderfully touching to be privy to Damiel's musings about what it must be like to become really real, to experience surprise, to feel the cold, to hold an apple, to be touched, to take the one he is falling in love with in his arms. As he observes our human ways his desire grows stronger. One day he finally crosses over and becomes flesh. Like a baby, or a just-dropped calf, he struggles to keep his physical balance. It is a moment of pure discovery. He runs. He skips. Grinning broadly he breathes deeply and feels his mouth; he rubs his hands together, making little sounds like 'Ah!' and 'Oh!'. Accidentally he bangs his head and, fascinated, he stares at the blood on his fingers and tastes it with delight. 'Is this what red is?' he asks a passer-by.

Like a child opening his presents on Christmas morning, Damiel reels and rocks under the delightful experience of each of his senses. He is ecstatic in his newly found humanity. His friendship with Marian grows stronger. By now the film is all in colour. The infectious exuberance of the angel made human, whether sucking on an ice cream, splashing in a puddle or staring at the colour purple, is fired with the enthusiasm of a child's first wonder. You sense a simplicity and an innocence in his delight at being alive, in his appetite for new experiences, especially the experience of loving someone. 'It is the love between us that has made me human,' Damiel reflects. 'That night I learned to be astonished. I now know what no other angel knows.'

The child in California wondered whether God enjoyed becoming a baby. Maybe the love story of Damiel is an echo of the love story of God. Maybe God, too, in the beginning, in the loneliness of infinity, yearned for playmates. 'God is sheer joy,' wrote St Thomas Aquinas, 'and sheer joy demands companionship.'

Could it be that God created the world in the first place because of a burning desire to be exactly like one of us, and so, to experience everything that human beings experience? Just as the committed love between women and men creates the new life of a baby, so too, the divine essence of extravagant and unconditional longing for human love gives birth to the world and to everything and everyone in it.

'God possesses the heavens,' wrote W. B. Yeats, 'but he covets the earth. Oh! ... he covets the earth.' Von Balthasar, the 'theologian of beauty', wrote about Incarnation as the fleshing out of 'God's eros, God's jealous, ravenous and loving desire for us.'

Imagination is the key to unlocking the undreamed-of beauty that lies behind the question of that wondering child. It was from the untamed wildness in her heart that her quiet reflection came. She was able to form it before we told her the wrong answers, before we boxed shut her creative soul and locked up her wild wonder. Her musings came straight from the divine imagination, still fresh as a daisy in her childhood essence. She sensed the impatience of God with divine invisibility: the need of God to be seen and heard.

Unfortunately, our preoccupation with the secondary issues

of the season blinds us to the many-splendoured thing at its centre. With unseeing hearts, we miss the shattering and shocking revelation of the crib.

I do not know what the child's father might have said to her. Very little, I hope. Still free, her untouched soul was already moving unerringly and more deeply into the beautiful mystery. In her small heart she may well have continued to wonder whether God longed for the playful experience of being the body and soul of everything – of all shapes and sizes, all colours and textures, all levels of life and all shades of imperfection. Maybe she was wondering whether God, the author of difference, the artist of transformation, longed to experience what it was like to change – from small to bigger to big, like acorns that grow huge, like tadpoles that become frogs, like baby snakes that stretch long, and small giraffes that reach tall, and like babies of every colour that beam brighter and bonnier with each passing day.

We ourselves, one of these misty evenings, need only tune in to the *puella aeterna* in our own souls, to hear the same questions. Did God come to us on the wings of desire, not reluctantly and with regret, as we were often told? Did God come to us with a passion for our human senses, to see and be seen, to touch and be touched, to understand and to be understood? Did God yearn to fall in love in a human way, to feel the shock of forgiveness, to say 'I believe in you', to be transfigured by courage and to shed the blood of fear?

This brings a final question: did God the Mother, in her sheer joy at becoming a baby, desire also the consequences of her planned vulnerability – that her outrageous love would soon lead her down that Jerusalem road, and up that Calvary hill, where a terrible cross of despair was being prepared for her in the broken body and tormented soul of her beloved, grown-up child?

'I wonder if God enjoys being a baby', our small mystic reflected beneath the fixed star and the floating angels. As her heart was still and silent before the mystery, did she begin to sense that she herself was that baby, that she too shone with the same light, that her own young body and heart were home to a delighted God, and that the winters of her life would always reveal an inevitable spring? And was this miracle true of every-one? Were we all, unknowingly, as full of God's beauty as the baby was? And if we really believed that all of this is true, how do we keep hurting each other, and destroying peace, like we do? How could anything ever be the same again?

Dear reader, maybe this is the Christmas when we allow our-selves, like God and like the young girl in our story, to be aston-ished at what we have taken for granted for far too long: to be deeply transformed by our new vision of the dark beauty and bright wonder of the divine humanity we are all graced with.

Breeze that blows open the heart

A sacramental vision sees every moments as a tiny incarnation of heaven's promise

There is a good chance that *The Shawshank Redemption* will be on television again this Christmas. It is a marvellous film, with a particularly memorable scene. Andy Dufresne is in prison for allegedly killing his wife, and because of his striking personality and presence he earns the respect of the warden who puts him in charge of the library. One day, while sorting out some books, Andy comes across an old 78 rpm recording of Mozart's *The Marriage of Figaro*. While the guard is distracted, the prisoner locks the door, puts the record on the player, flicks on the prison sound system, and the beautiful duettino *Sull'aria* flows out and fills the whole compound – a compound of grey shadows and hard noises.

All over the prison yard the empty faces of men are lifted up to the speakers as the music surges across the bleak spaces of institutional harshness and starving human hearts. Who knows what powerful images and emotions surfaced in their souls during those four timeless minutes of transformation? Maybe some ached at the memory of a lost heaven – of a loving family, a promising job, a real respect, because of one careless risk. The eyes of others may have grown moist at the mistakes made, in desperation perhaps, to acquire money to impress a demanding lover. Yet others may have been remembering a golden childhood moment, or their mother.

'Those two voices', the narrator explains, 'were singing about something so beautiful that it cannot be expressed in words, higher than anybody in this dead place dares to dream. It was like some beautiful bird descended into our drab little cage making those hard, black walls dissolve away – and for the briefest moment every last man at Shawshank felt free.'

Andy himself said, 'You need music so you don't forget that there is something deep within you that they cannot get to, that they cannot touch, something that is always truly yours – I'm talking about possibility.'

There are times in our own imperfect lives when the veil parts between the two worlds we contain – our inner desire for a more divine destiny and the hard reality of our present circumstances. Like the music over the prison plant, something unforeseen hijacks our unfocused spirit. In *Postscript*, Seamus Heaney writes about the sideways breeze off the ocean that catches us off guard and blows our heart wide open. Such sacramental glimpses have a baptismal edge to them, marking us forever.

Brian Friel's play *Dancing at Lughnasa* features five unfulfilled sisters in their Co Donegal cottage in 1936. It is the time of the annual Celtic harvest festival named after the pagan god Lugh. Things are not good. Disgrace and penury are killing their stifled souls. But dancing is the key metaphor of the play. In a most extraordinary burst of ecstasy, the five women release their emotional and sexual suppression by dancing to a reel issuing from their new-fangled wireless. It is a glimpse of the unquenchable passions that come from far beyond words, far beyond the sisters' kitchen. Some kind of sacramental shutter was thrown open for a moment, and in swept the uncontrollable but necessary wildness that lies just below the surface of our barely civilised souls.

Teilhard de Chardin offers us a superb example of what is meant by the Catholic imagination:

O Lord, since I have neither bread nor wine nor altar here on the Asian steppes, I lift myself far above symbols, to the pure majesty of the Real; and I, your priest, offer to you on the altar of the entire earth, the travail and suffering of the world. Yonder breaks the sun, to light the uttermost east, and then to send its sheets of fire over the living surface of the earth, which wakens, shudders and resumes its relentless struggle. My paten and my chalice are the depths of a soul laid widely open to all the forces which in a moment will rise up from every corner of the earth and converge upon the Spirit.

There are smaller epiphanies, too, of the underlying reality of our lives. I like to think of the Angelus as a small Christmas, a revelation of the colour at the heart of our monochrome world. The bell rings and we are called to place our hearts where our hands are busy. As at Eucharist-time, we are not invited to move into a sacred place, removed from the distractions of the daily grind, but, with holy imagination, to experience the deeper graces lying within what we may call menial or routine. Beyond a passing celebration of Christmas, this way of being is a daily participation in Incarnation; it is called eucharistic living.

There is a Teilhard in everyone – waiting for, and recognising, the beyond in our midst. This is Advent time, and it is forever. We are perennially called to be God's mystics as we search for God's traces everywhere; diviners who detect the holy water of life in the soil of our being; persistent beachcombers seeking the glimmer of God's gold on the shores of our souls.

These almost subliminal but breathtaking glimpses are all tiny incarnations of heaven's promise. Without them we forget and lose the way – the way of truly seeing. 'We could dream the world,' wrote Daniel Berrigan, 'we could dream the eye. But who can imagine the act of seeing? We will never have enough of this; we will never have done with it.' And why? Because each such moment of insight is, in the words of R. S. Thomas, the small, bright field with the buried treasure. These unrepeatable, vagrant moments hold the memory and the hope of our source and destiny:

It is the turning
aside like Moses to the miracle
of the lit bush, to a brightness
that seemed as transitory as your youth
once, but is the eternity that awaits you.

Whether it be the redemption at Shawshank, the Angelus in the kitchen, the wild dance across the fields of Ballybeg, the Eucharist over the world, or any of the countless daily graces that enable us to see into, and beyond, the immediate reality, transcending and transforming it into a new creation, they are all sustained and intensified by those two greatest sacraments of the heart – that first morning when the huge heart of the Creator spun the earth lovingly into being; and then, that enduring night when God's astonishing desire for us was revealed in the small heart of a starry-eyed and mystified child whom Christians call Jesus.

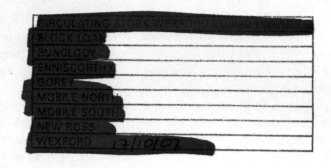

CIRCULATING STOCK WEXFORD PUBLIC LIBRARY

BLOCK LOAN	

BUNCLODY	
ENNISCORTHY	
GOREY	
MOBILE NORTH	
MOBILE SOUTH	
NEW ROSS	
WEXFORD 17/10/07	

LAST IN CIRC:
17/02/20